# *Flow*

## Reading Without Borders

James Baron　Joe Henley

SEIBIDO

**photographs by**

iStockphoto

Shutterstock

Imaginechina/時事通信フォト

EPA＝時事

**音声ファイルのダウンロード／ストリーミング**

CD マーク表示がある箇所は、音声を弊社 HP より無料でダウンロード／ストリーミングすることができます。 下記 URL の書籍詳細ページに音声ダウンロードアイコンがございますのでそちらから自習用音声としてご活用ください。

http://seibido.co.jp/ad671

**Flow: Reading Without Borders**

# Contents

# Content Chart

| | Type of Reading | Title | Reading Skill | Vocabulary Builder |
|---|---|---|---|---|
| **Unit 1** | Online Forum | Does a Sloth Make a Good Pet? | Scanning for Personal Opinions | The Prefix *in-* |
| **Unit 2** | Letter | Why People Say "Yes" to Late Marriage | Using Context Clues | The Suffix *-ize* |
| **Unit 3** | Web Article (1) | Spotify: A Singing Success | Skimming for Typographical Cues | The Prefix *fore-* |
| **Unit 4** | Folk Tale | Why Do Dogs Chase Cats? | Identifying Character Traits | The Suffix *-en* |
| **Unit 5** | Environmental Article | The Man Who Grew a Forest | Guessing the Meaning of Unfamiliar Vocabulary | The Suffixes *-ery* and *-ry* |
| **Unit 6** | Advertisement | Find Your Dream Job Today | Recognizing an Author's Motivation | The Prefix *sub-* |

**Review 1**

# Learning Overview

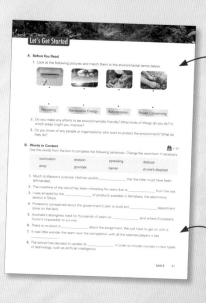

## Let's Get Started

**Let's Get Started** introduces the reading topic of each unit with an interesting warm-up activity.

## Words in Context

**Words in Context** is a fill-in-the-blank exercise which helps students study key words from the reading.

## Reading

Different types of **Reading** lead students to a wide range of modern topics and useful key words. There are also Notes that help students understand difficult words.

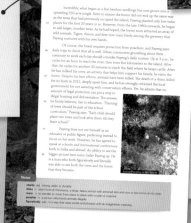

## Reading Comprehension

**Reading Comprehension** helps check whether students have understood the text entirely by testing on purposes, details, inferences, etc.

## Think More

**Think More** provides two additional questions for discussion to enhance students' critical thinking skills.

## ▶ Reading Skill

**Reading Skill** teaches skimming, scanning, etc. Task 1 helps students practice the newly learned skill, and Task 2 shows students how to apply the skill to the reading.

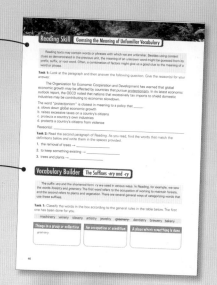

## ▶ Vocabulary Builder

**Vocabulary Builder** introduces useful mechanics of English words such as prefixes and suffixes.

## ▶ Let's Think About It!

**Let's Think About It!** incorporates four learning skills that are crucial to success in the modern world: Communication, Collaboration, Creativity, and Critical Thinking.

## ▶ Review

**Review** contains four types of questions: Definition Matching, Sentence Completion, Cloze Test, and Reading Comprehension.

# Does a Sloth Make a Good Pet?

## Let's Get Started

### A. Before You Read

1. Look at the following animals and match them to their names.

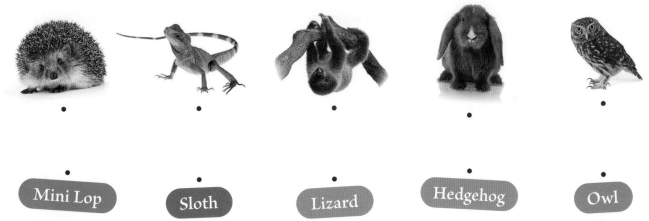

Mini Lop • Sloth • Lizard • Hedgehog • Owl

2. Do you think these animals above are suitable for keeping as pets? Choose two animals that you would keep as pets and give your reasons.

3. Do you have a pet? If you do, what is it and why do you have it as a pet? If you don't, what pet do you want to get?

### B. Words in Context

 1-02

Use the words from the box to complete the following sentences. Change the word form if necessary.

| | | | |
|---|---|---|---|
| collective | humid | consciousness | obsessed |
| comprehend | habitat | definitely | companionship |

1. Jenny's young daughter is currently _____ with a cartoon called *Peppa Pig*.

2. Hollywood actors and actresses can easily enter the public _____ but can just as easily be forgotten.

3. Over-development in the mountains has destroyed the natural _____ of many animals.

4. I cannot _____ why anyone would do such a terrible thing to that nice family.

5. We decided to make a(n) _____ decision on the important matter that affected us all.

6. Look at those dark clouds in the sky over there; it is _____ going to start raining soon!

7. The weather in Japan in the summer is usually very hot and _____.

8. The elderly lady enjoys the _____ that her cats provide her with.

1-03~07

---

**Nov 27, 2021**                                              #1

**CharloCY**

Join Date:
Nov 2017
Posts: 12

I watched the animated movie *Zootopia* and became so obsessed with one of the supporting characters—the sloth working in the office. After that, I went on to the *Ice Age* series. Sid the Sloth was adorable in an ugly sort of way. He had a cute little speech impediment, and he was incredibly clumsy. But there was also something endearing about him. He was unfailingly kind and loyal. From that point on, sloths have never been far from my mind.

Because of my love of this animal, I'm interested in raising one on my own. A few years ago, I was a pretty inattentive kid, but now I'm financially independent and live in my own house with a big backyard. I think I'm ready to get a pet now, and my one and only choice is definitely a sloth!

Would anyone be willing to share any information about getting a sloth as a pet? Thanks!

---

**Nov 27, 2021**                                              #2

**Beaky0506**

Join Date:
Nov 2014
Posts: 61

I understand that you want to have a pet that you will love, and I'm sure your pet will provide you with the companionship that you need. But I don't think learning about an animal only from movies is a good idea. If you had done some basic research on sloths, you would comprehend that they do not make good pets.

Generally speaking, a sloth is an exotic animal that only lives in some parts of South America and Central America. A sloth basically lives in trees. It has a very low body temperature, so it is unable to stand the cold. So, if you really want to get a sloth, you will need to spend quite a lot of time and money to build a warm

---

**Notes**

**impediment** *n.* a condition that makes it difficult for someone to do something such as speaking
**clumsy** *adj.* moving or doing things in a way that is not careful or graceful
**endearing** *adj.* inspiring affection

and humid environment for it. You will also need to plant a lot of trees for it to climb. 30

Next, a sloth likes to eat fresh leaves and fruits, so you'll have to grow these things or provide them for your pet sloth. This is not an easy job. 35 Besides, the digestive system of a sloth is also very SLOW. Your pet sloth may need a few weeks or even a month to digest one meal!

A sloth is cute, but I seriously doubt that it will be a good pet. I hope you think twice before you get one. 40

**Nov 28, 2021** #3

**Min<3Bella**

Join Date:
Mar 2013
Posts: 26

I remember a few months back everyone was really into owls. I believe it started when people in the West suddenly became aware of owl cafés in Japan—places where people can sit and enjoy a cup of coffee with a tiny owl for company. I admit that I, too, was taken in by the allure 50 of this trend for a short while, but I've never wanted to really keep an owl as a pet. 45

I think that we are interested in these special animals mostly because we are not familiar with them. Actually, I would suggest that you get a cat or a dog now that you have a big 55 backyard! Cats and dogs are lovely, and you can build a real relationship with them. You also have more resources available to take care of them.

**Notes**

**digestive** *adj.* things related to digestion, which is the process of food passing through the body
**allure** *n.* the quality of being mysteriously attractive

**SnowTK**

Join Date:
May 2016
Posts: 22

Sloths are tropical mammals. Their claws are so long that they have difficulty walking on the ground. They also spend most of their time sleeping and hanging from branches in trees.

In some states in America, it is against the law to keep a sloth as a pet. What if you were attacked or injured by one? The sloth could be infested with parasites, and you may develop a serious infection if you are injured by it. In short, sloths should live in the wild, not in your home.

**CharloCY**

Join Date:
Nov 2017
Posts: 13

Thanks for all the comments. I did some research on the Internet, and then my desire to get a sloth as a pet died down. I also would not want to buy a sloth because of what I learned about animal trafficking.

Yet, I think using a sloth as a cartoon character puts it into the collective consciousness of people who normally might not think about this animal at all. This helps draw attention to conservation groups and sanctuaries such as The Sloth Sanctuary and Slothville, which provide safe habitats for sloths in areas where their normal abodes might be threatened by encroachment by humans. Nowadays, people are becoming more and more educated about sloths and finding out about their naturally friendly manner. I can only hope that this trend will continue and that we can go on to provide even more care and protection for this animal.

## Notes

**infest**  *v.*  (of creatures) to be present in large numbers and often cause damage
**trafficking**  *n.*  the illegal trade of certain things, such as drugs, stolen items, or people
**sanctuary**  *n.*  a place where a person or animal is safe from enemies or attackers
**abode**  *n.*  a place where a person or animal lives
**encroachment**  *n.*  movement into territory that belongs to others

# Reading Comprehension

**Multiple Choice:** Based on the reading, choose the best answer to each question.

DETAIL
1. What do we know from the first post?
   a. CharloCY seldom watches animated movies.
   b. CharloCY is interested in getting a pet.
   c. CharloCY wants to invite people to watch *Ice Age*.
   d. *Zootopia* is a movie about sloths.

VOCABULARY
2. In Line 6, the word "unfailingly" is closest in meaning to _____.
   a. successfully
   b. immediately
   c. always
   d. never

DETAIL
3. Based on the second post, what do we know about a sloth?
   a. Its skin is very wet.
   b. It enjoys eating parasites.
   c. It is able to survive in cold places.
   d. Its eating habits require special care.

INFERENCE
4. What did Min<3Bella imply in the post?
   a. A sloth may not develop a relationship with humans.
   b. CharloCY should get an owl instead.
   c. Keeping a sloth is a very good idea.
   d. There should be a sloth café.

REFERENCE
5. What does the word "one" refer to in Line 64?
   a. A tropical mammal
   b. A parasite
   c. A sloth
   d. An injury

PREDICTION
6. What will CharloCY do after reading all of the posts?
   a. He or she will find a way to use animal trafficking.
   b. He or she will keep on caring about sloths.
   c. He or she will keep a sloth.
   d. He or she will go to visit Slothville.

**Think More**

1. What do you know about sloths? Do you like them? Why or why not?

2. Have you ever had an obsession with a certain kind of animal? What was it, and why were you so interested in it?

# Reading Skill  Scanning for Personal Opinions

Sometimes in an article or a piece of reading text, the author offers personal opinions on a certain topic. As we read, we learn to recognize the author's attitude toward the topic, whether it's positive, negative, ambivalent, or critical.

**Task 1:** Read the following short passage and underline the author's personal opinion(s).

I was not really into owls. One day after work, I passed by a so-called "owl café." Out of curiosity, I stepped in because I wanted to know why it was so popular these days. I saw about 15 owls in the room. Some were big, some were small, some looked sleepy, while some seemed quite alert. The owner told me that I could try to stroke one small owl, so I did. It was amazing! The owl was really cute and sweet. From then on, the owl café became a healing place whenever I needed to relax.

**Task 2:** Scan the second post in Reading and answer the questions.

1. Which of the following is Beaky0506's personal opinion?
   a. Sloths only live in some parts of South America.
   b. Providing sloths with food is not an easy job.
   c. Sloths can't stand the cold.
   d. The digestive system of a sloth is very slow.

2. Beaky0506's attitude toward keeping a sloth is _____.
   a. positive
   b. ambivalent
   c. optimistic
   d. negative

# Vocabulary Builder  The Prefix *in-*

The prefix *in-* means "the opposite of" or "not," and it is used to form negative words in English. It can be used with adjectives, adverbs, and nouns. In Reading, we saw the examples *independent* and *inattentive*, the former meaning "not dependent" and the latter meaning "not attentive."

**Task 1:** Which of the following words can take the prefix *in-*? Write the prefix in the space for those which can take it or put an "X" in front of the words which can't.

1. _____sensitive

2. _____action

3. _____attractive

4. _____happiness

5. _____flexibility

6. _____complicated

7. _____capable

8. _____accurately

**Task 2:** Use the words from the box to complete the passage.

| indefensible | inescapable | inexpensive | inappropriate | inorganic |

   Morgan went to the supermarket, looking for some (1)_____ produce. She needed to save money, but she wanted to eat healthily as well. She soon found that the cheapest vegetables were (2)_____. That means they may have been grown using many chemicals. If she wanted to buy organic food, high prices were (3)_____. Morgan thought that this was (4)_____. Why should healthy food be out of reach for people who have a low income? She went to speak to the manager about what she felt was an (5)_____ pricing scheme. The manager, however, merely said he would look into it.

# Let's Think About It!

   The number of endangered animal species continues to grow. This includes two of the six species of sloths. The table below shows some of the causes. Working in pairs, look at each cause in the table and think about what we can do to protect animal species. You can also list other causes and discuss them with your partner. You may do some online research if necessary.

| Causes | What we can do |
|---|---|
| Climate change (Global warming) | • Set temperature of air-conditioners at moderate to cut $CO_2$ emissions |
| Environmental pollution | |
| Invasive species | |
| | |

# Why People Say "Yes" to Late Marriage

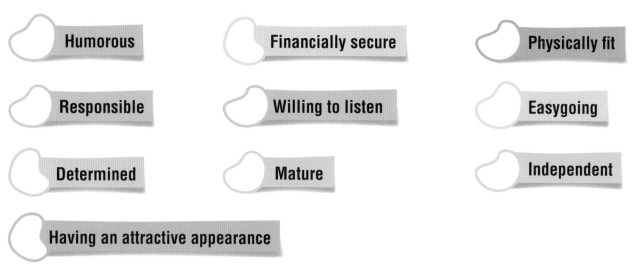

## Let's Get Started

### A. Before You Read

1. Do you have an image of your ideal future partner? Check the five traits that you think are most important for him or her to have.

- ⬡ **Humorous**
- ⬡ **Financially secure**
- ⬡ **Physically fit**
- ⬡ **Responsible**
- ⬡ **Willing to listen**
- ⬡ **Easygoing**
- ⬡ **Determined**
- ⬡ **Mature**
- ⬡ **Independent**
- ⬡ **Having an attractive appearance**

2. If you met your ideal partner, when do you think would be the best age to get married? With a partner, share the reasons for your decision.

### B. Words in Context   1-08

Use the words from the box to complete the following sentences. Change the word form if necessary.

| | | | |
|---|---|---|---|
| solid | awareness | roll around | footing |
| consequence | workforce | cohabitation | counterpart |

1. Although we know that the new law will be passed soon, we still do not know what its _____ will be.

2. Some people believe that _____ before marriage is a sin.

3. The new program is trying to raise _____ among young people of the dangers of global warming.

4. I will contact my _____ in our New York office to find out how to handle this problem.

5. Good communication is the key to building a(n) _____ relationship with your spouse.

6. According to a recent report, most of the _____ is employed in that country.

7. Our company is very fair, and in our office, you can compete with others on equal _____.

8. We should be ready with a new sales program when the new year _____.

CD 1-09~14

Dear Editor,

I'm writing to respond to the July 23rd article by Dr. Trampson, in which he stated that he believes early marriage is a popular idea today. I would like to tell him that, as a matter of fact, late marriage is the trend in the US nowadays. Men and
5 women, it seems, are currently choosing to get married later in life than they did in years past. Recently, I had a look at a census chart which showed marriage statistics from 1890 to 2021, and here are a few basic facts. In 1890, men tended to get married at about 26 years of age. Women, on the other hand, were around 22 when they tied the knot. By the time 1950 rolled around, women walked down the aisle
10 at age 20, while men took the plunge at 23. Since then, however, Americans have been waiting longer and longer to say "I do." In fact, today men get married at an average of 30 years of age, while women are slightly younger at 28.

In my opinion, this happens for many reasons. For starters, more and more couples now decide to live together before choosing whether or not to formalize
15 their relationship in the eyes of the law. Back in the 1950s, the practice of cohabitation was considered taboo and even sinful. However, most people today would not bat an eye at a couple who choose to live together outside of marriage. Today, nearly 48 percent of women in the US choose to live with their partners rather than putting on a wedding
20 ring, according to the National Center for Health Statistics report.

There are other factors at play in people delaying marriage. One is that more people are
25 choosing to live alone for longer periods of time. It used to be that men and women would finish school, get married, and move in with their partner right away.
30 Those days are gone, especially as women have fought to win equal

The practice of cohabitation

## Notes

**census** *n.* an official survey of the people of a country
**take the plunge** *idiom* to commit oneself to doing something risky; to get married
**sinful** *adj.* morally wrong or bad

Today, women put more focus on developing their potential in their jobs.

footing in college and the workplace with their male counterparts. These days, women are just as likely to go to college and enter the workforce as men, whereas in times past they were more mothers and homemakers. Being more independent today, women now make developing their own potential and confidence a top priority. With increased options before them, women are naturally deciding to put marriage on the back burner.

35

Now, this brings us to the consequences of this trend. What does putting marriage off mean for both men and women? For women, it seems, the outcome is largely positive in terms of their career and earning potential. For example, a woman who chooses to go to university and marry in her thirties will, according to statistics, earn $15,000 per year more than a woman who marries in her early twenties. Interestingly, however, the effect of delaying marriage on men seems to be the opposite. Even college-educated men, studies show, will earn less, on average, if they choose to marry in their thirties rather than in their twenties.

40

45

Of course, we can't deny that family relationships are important in society, but entering into marriage is such a life-changing decision that we should take time to think about it carefully. Besides, marriage is not the only way to form a solid and healthy family relationship. Some people do not even think getting married is a necessary step in their lives.

50

## Notes

**homemaker** *n.* someone who takes care of the house and family as their main job
**put ... on the back burner** *idiom* to stop doing something or dealing with someone or something (less important)

More and more people tend to get married late.

Frankly speaking, the age that people marry isn't really something we as a society at large can control, nor should we strive to control it. Rather, we should raise awareness of self-development and let young people decide for themselves when the time is right to make a lifelong, legal commitment to a partner. When it

55  comes down to it, I strongly believe that being a responsible person is far more important than getting married early.

Sincerely,
Wayne Beckett
Daly City, California

# Reading Comprehension

**Multiple Choice:** Based on the reading, choose the best answer to each question.

PURPOSE
1. What is the purpose of this letter?
   a. To exhibit the benefits of getting married at a young age
   b. To agree with Dr. Trampson's article
   c. To illustrate why late marriage is harmful
   d. To show how late marriage is the current trend

DETAIL
2. What do we know about men and women from 1890 to 1950?
   a. They tended to get married at a younger age.
   b. Women got married at an older age than men.
   c. Men wanted to wait longer before they got married.
   d. They enjoyed the practice of living together before getting married.

DETAIL
3. What do people nowadays think about cohabitation?
   a. They despise those who do it.
   b. They think it's a necessary step before marriage.
   c. They hold a liberal attitude toward it.
   d. They encourage young people to do it.

DETAIL
4. Which of the following is a reason why people today are choosing to delay marriage?
   a. They want to live with their parents longer.
   b. They want to try experiencing life with different partners.
   c. They choose to live alone for a longer period of time.
   d. They do not trust the system of marriage.

DETAIL
5. Based on the fifth paragraph, which of the following is true?
   a. We can only build a family relationship by getting married.
   b. Getting married is a very important decision in people's lives.
   c. Every person needs to get married at least once in their lives.
   d. If you spend too much time considering marriage, you are not suitable for marriage.

INFERENCE
6. Which of the following can be inferred from the article?
   a. It is difficult to objectively analyze the overall costs of getting married.
   b. No matter when you get married, it will help you to earn more money.
   c. Men and women should get married.
   d. Late marriage tends to benefit women financially more than men.

## Think More

1. Can you think of any disadvantages of getting married late?

2. What do you think the impact on society will be if more and more people get married late?

# Reading Skill (Using Context Clues)

In an article, there may be words or phrases that we have never learned before. To understand the meanings these words or phrases, the ability to use context clues is a useful skill. **Definitions**, **examples**, **synonyms**, and even **antonyms** often surround the unknown words or are in the same sentence, and they are the clues we can use when we read a text. We may not figure out the exact meaning of the unknown parts of a sentence or phrase, but through these context clues, we can gain a better understanding of these difficult portions.

**Task 1:** Read the following sentences. Then, write down the types of the context clues and the meaning of the underlined words. The first one has been done for you.

1. Stop <u>pestering</u> and annoying me while I study. I really have an important exam tomorrow!

   Type of context clue: _synonym_          Meaning of the underlined word: _annoy_

2. There are some new regulations for the <u>matriculation</u>, which is the process of enrolling, in our university. Students who fail to meet the requirements may not be accepted by us.

   Type of context clue: _____          Meaning of the underlined word: _____

3. Fiona is <u>reticent</u> about her boyfriend. For instance, she never shows his pictures to anyone.

   Type of context clue: _____          Meaning of the underlined word: _____

**Task 2:** Look at the following passage from Reading. What do the marked phrases mean, and how do you know? Underline the context clues and write down the meanings of the two phrases.

In 1890, men tended to get married at about 26 years of age. Women, on the other hand, were around 22 when they **tied the knot**. By the time 1950 rolled around, women **walked down the aisle** at age 20, while men took the plunge at 23.

tie the knot: _____

walk down the aisle: _____

# Vocabulary Builder (The Suffix *-ize*)

The suffix *-ize* is added to nouns or adjectives in order to form verbs which generally tend to have the meaning of making or converting something in a certain way. In Reading, for example, we saw the verb *formalize*, which means to make something formal.

**Task 1:** Match the words to the correct definitions.

1. legalize           •                     • to make a government-owned business private
2. privatize          •                     • (of a country or area) to develop many industries
3. industrialize      •                     • to make something become a fossil
4. itemize            •                     • to make something legal
5. fossilize          •                     • to make a list of things in detail

**Task 2:** Choose a word from the box to complete the sentences. Change the word form if necessary.

| characterize | liquidize | finalize | modernize |
|---|---|---|---|

1. Peter's company spent about $50,000 on _____ its computer system.

2. A capital is often _____ as being the biggest city in a country. However, in some countries, this is not the case.

3. To make a smoothie, Joanne _____ the fruits and mixed them together.

4. We need more time to _____ the details of the agreement.

## Let's Think About It!

In this unit, we read about a current social trend that has the potential to have a deep impact not just on the place in which it is happening, but on the world as a whole. Now, let's see if we can determine the root causes of the trend as well as a few others, and then come up with some possible solutions to these potential problems.

In groups of four to six, look at the trends listed below and try to come up with their root causes and possible solutions. You can also list a social trend that you want to discuss with the members of your group.

| Trend | Root Causes | Possible Solutions |
|---|---|---|
| Delayed marriage | • Increased focus on career | |
| Delayed home ownership | • A rise in temporary employment | |
| Delay in having children | | • Government subsidies for those who have newborns |
| Delay in finding a job after graduation | | |
| | | |

Spotify:
# A Singing Success

## Let's Get Started

### A. Before You Read

1. What are some streaming services used in Japan? Which one(s) do you use?

2. Think of the advantages and disadvantages of streaming music and list them in the chart below.

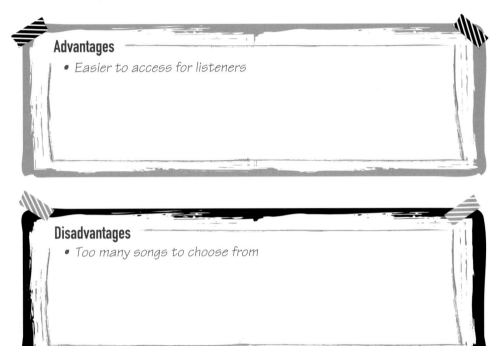

**Advantages**
- Easier to access for listeners

**Disadvantages**
- Too many songs to choose from

### B. Words in Context

 1-15

Use the words from the box to complete the following sentences. Change the word form if necessary.

| | | | |
|---|---|---|---|
| server | accessible | royalty | setback |
| mark | follow suit | immensely | compile |

1. Lorde is a(n) _____ popular star whose songs have captured the hearts of millions of fans.

2. I can't get on the Internet right now. Could there be a problem with the _____?

3. _____ paid to the singer for streams of her songs last year topped $50,000.

4. After experiencing one _____ after another, the business was forced to close its doors.

5. Mr. Robinson will _____ a list of all the candidates who are up for the promotion.

6. After the popular manager announced that she was leaving the company, several others in the company decided to _____ and leave the company, as well.

7. In 2021, the number of Facebook users worldwide reached the 2.9 billion _____.

8. All of the information about the new product is easily _____ on the Internet.

1-16~24

The digital age of music has caused songs, albums, and singles to go through rapid changes. When MP3s first became available, the online realm was like the Wild West. Almost everything was accessible, and many people chose to stop buying music in stores. Instead, they turned to downloading copies of their favorite
5　artists' songs and releases*. Those days of piracy are far from gone and forgotten, but thanks to Spotify, previewing an album before you buy, or just listening to it online, has never been easier or more guilt-free.

　　As big as Spotify is, it started out as just a couple of guys brainstorming in a small apartment. Daniel Ek and Martin Lorentzon first started working on the idea
10　that would become Spotify at Ek's place in 2005, with Lorentzon sleeping on a bare mattress on the floor. The heat from all the Internet servers they had running in the tiny space was so great that the pair of them often worked half-naked.

　　All that hard work and sweat paid off in 2006 when Spotify was officially founded in Stockholm, Sweden. By the spring of the following year, the first beta
15　version of the nascent streaming service was available to the public. The founders had to figure out a way to publicize Spotify. One way they came up with was allowing users to compile their own playlists of their favorite singers and tracks, and then allowing them to share these lists. This was one of the factors that helped Spotify to go viral.

20　　At first, Spotify was ad-free, but by 2008 Ek and Lorentzon realized that the way forward would be paid with advertising revenue and private investment. In its first round of funding, the company managed to
25　raise over US$21 million. This was just the beginning. In 2008, the beta version of Spotify was replaced with the first official version, attracting hundreds of thousands of users, not

* Most music-sharing sites were illegal at the time.

## Notes

**piracy**  *n.*  the crime of illegally using or reproducing someone's work
**nascent**  *adj.*  just coming into existence and displaying potential
**publicize**  *v.*  to make something widely known
**go viral**  *idiom*  to become very popular, often by being shared by many people on the Internet

Spotify allows online users to share their playlists.

to mention tens of millions more in investments into the company.          30

This is not to say that the launch of Spotify was without roadblocks. In the spring of 2009, the service hit its first major challenge with a data leak that could have potentially made private user information public. However, the company was able to overcome the setback and used investor money to pay off record labels for their artist catalogs, thus putting more music on Spotify than ever before. In those          35 days, not everyone was sold on streaming. Labels and artists were concerned about how they would get paid for the content they were providing. Advanced payments from Spotify helped to lower their level of concern.

By 2011, the number of Spotify users topped the one million mark, and the service, only available in the European Union to this point, was officially launched          40 in the US. The founders announced a partnership with Facebook, whose founder, Mark Zuckerberg, had previously expressed his enthusiasm for the service. Now, Spotify users could automatically share their Spotify activities via the immensely popular social network. Investments continued to pour in as the music industry and music lovers gradually developed the habit of using streaming services. In the          45

winter of 2013, it was announced that Spotify had more than 24 million users who had streamed 4.5 billion hours worth of music in that year alone.

Facebook was only the start of          50 Spotify's creative use of partnerships and tie-ins. In 2014, Ek and Lorentzon saw ride-sharing app Uber grow in popularity, so they acted quickly to take

## Notes

**roadblock**  *n.*  something that stops you from moving forward
**tie-in**  *n.*  a product that is marketed, promoted, or sold with another product

Spotify users were able to "stream" their music in a Uber car.

55    advantage of this opportunity. Spotify Premium users* were able to "stream" their music in Uber cars, so they could enjoy their own tunes when going from point A to point B.

Though fans were reportedly delighted with Spotify and its ever-evolving platform, some artists expressed their displeasure with the low royalties offered by
60    the service. Pop sensation Taylor Swift, for example, pulled all her songs from Spotify in 2014. Other high-profile singers soon followed suit. This, however, did little to slow the company's progress. Some artists eventually came back as they came to realize that the streaming trend is unstoppable. Spotify has since spawned several imitators, all looking to cash in on the huge popularity of streaming.

65    In 2015, Apple launched Apple Music, which was meant to compete directly with Spotify. Spotify, however, remains at the top of the heap. The service has over 190 million paid subscribers. And, in spite of protests from the likes of Taylor Swift, Spotify points out that it has paid out more than US$30 billion in royalties to artists. Love it or hate it, streaming and Spotify go hand in hand. Spotify has
70    outlasted its file-sharing forerunners, such as Napster, and now it even counts Napster founder Sean Parker as an investor. One thing is for certain, neither streaming music nor Spotify seems to be going anywhere anytime soon.

---

* These are the users who paid for a premium service to enjoy ad-free streaming.

### Notes

**reportedly**   *adv.*  according to what people say
**spawn**   *v.*  to produce or generate something new
**imitator**   *n.*  someone who tries to copy someone or something
**outlast**   *v.*  to live or exist longer than other things

# Reading Comprehension

**Multiple Choice:** Based on the reading, choose the best answer to each question.

PURPOSE  **1.** What is the main purpose of this article?

   a. It talks about different ways artists are promoting their music today.

   b. It shows how the music industry has failed to evolve with the times.

   c. It compares and contrasts several music streaming services.

   d. It presents the history of a revolutionary service.

INFERENCE  **2.** What can be inferred about the time when MP3s first became available?

   a. No one wanted MP3s unless they could get them legally.

   b. Every song ever recorded was instantly available.

   c. Few people showed interest in the new invention.

   d. Many people downloaded tracks illegally.

DETAIL  **3.** What was decided in 2008?

   a. Spotify would launch in the United States.

   b. Spotify would do away with sharing playlists.

   c. Spotify would earn revenue through advertising.

   d. Spotify would always remain ad-free.

DETAIL  **4.** What were some labels and artists concerned about at first?

   a. How Spotify would make their content available

   b. How they would get paid from streaming

   c. When Spotify would be available in all regions

   d. Where Spotify would launch their songs

PARAPHRASE  **5.** What does the author mean by "not everyone was sold on streaming" in Line 36?

   a. Streaming was not as popular as live concerts.

   b. Streaming was favored by everyone.

   c. Some thought streaming was too expensive.

   d. Some didn't think streaming was a good idea.

DETAIL  **6.** What did Taylor Swift do in 2014?

   a. She took all her songs off Spotify.

   b. She announced a partnership with Spotify.

   c. She gave Spotify all her songs for free.

   d. She decided to take Spotify to court.

## Think More

1. If you were a singer, would you put your music on Spotify? Why or why not?

2. How do you think Spotify measures up against other streaming services?

## Reading Skill — Skimming for Typographical Cues

Skimming for typographical cues is a quick way to grasp some points that the author is trying to emphasize. Typographical cues are things like asterisks, italics, bold type, underlined words, quotation marks, etc. They could be indications that the words themselves or the surrounding text are of some significance to your overall understanding of the article's main points. Asterisks, for example, indicate that you will find more information in a footnote. Underlined words, quotation marks, bold type, or italics indicate that a word is relatively important or has a special meaning.

**Task 1:** Skim for the typographical cues in the following passage. Then, answer the following question.

Jerome had never been so embarrassed in his whole life. He had always been self-conscious about his looks. His wife always told him that it was difficult for strangers to judge his real age*. But when he dropped his daughter off on her first day of school, he was mortified. When he handed his daughter off to the teacher, she said sweetly, "Oh, it's so nice when a grandparent takes the time to take a grandchild to school." At that point, Jerome wished there was a nice, big rock he could just crawl under.

* He is 35 years old.

What is true about Jerome?
a. He is confident about his looks.
c. He looks much older than he truly is.
b. He and his daughter look alike.
d. He is embarrassed because of his wife.

**Task 2:** Skim through the seventh paragraph of Reading and answer the following questions.

1. Apart from ad-free listening, what benefit could Spotify Premium users enjoy?

_____

2. What do you think the word "stream" means in this paragraph?

_____

## Vocabulary Builder — The Prefix *fore-*

The prefix *fore-* indicates that something comes before something else. For example, a weather forecaster might *forecast* the weather, predicting a sunny day ahead. In Reading, we learned that Napster was on the market before Spotify, so Napster can be considered a *forerunner* of Spotify.

**Task 1:** Look at the following words and guess their meanings. Write down your definitions for these words.

1. foreword: _____

2. foremost: _____

3. forearm: _____

4. foretell: _____

5. foresight: _____

**Task 2:** Use the words from Task 1 to complete the following short passage. Not all of the words will be used.

Few people have the (1) _____ to predict future trends with consistent accuracy. There are a few, however, who are able to (2) _____ what might happen in the months, years, or even decades to come. Such people are called "futurists," and the most skilled ones are highly sought after as public speakers. Many have even published popular books, filled with their future predictions. One of the (3) _____ futurists is Bruce Sterling, a best-selling science-fiction author whose descriptions of the world of tomorrow have proven mysteriously accurate.

## Let's Think About It!

Below is a list of various streaming services and websites that could potentially help an artist in selling his or her music, or at least getting it heard. In a group, have a discussion about the pros and cons of each of the services. If you don't know much about a particular site or service, you may do some research online. Write them down in the chart below. Then, try to determine which one is the best of the bunch. Share your conclusions with the rest of the class.

| Streaming Services | Pros | Cons |
|---|---|---|
| **SPOTIFY** | *It has the largest number of registered users of any streaming service to date.* | *Royalty rates for each stream are quite low, and the large number of artists on the site make it difficult for artists to stand out in the crowd.* |
| **KKBOX** | | |
| **APPLE MUSIC** | | |
| **YOUTUBE** | | |
| **DEEZER** | | |

I think _____ is the best because _____.

# Why Do Dogs Chase Cats?

## Let's Get Started

### A. Before You Read

1. Look at the various kinds of animals here. Which ones do you believe would make good pets and why?

2. Of those you checked, what do you think they can do for humans?

3. Why do you think people feel the need to keep pets?

### B. Words in Context

🎵 1-25

Use the words from the box to complete the following sentences. Change the word form if necessary.

| | | | |
|---|---|---|---|
| oath | ordeal | banish | salvation |
| betrayal | doom | paddle | solemn |

1. Because Roger was under _____ in court, he had to tell the prosecutor everything he knew about the murder.

2. It's quite a(n) _____ to start a business from scratch and get it up and running.

3. A wedding vow is a(n) _____ promise to love another person for the rest of your life.

4. When the earthquake struck, our home's strong foundation was our only _____.

5. Mary couldn't bear her boyfriend's _____, so she broke up with him.

6. The boy doesn't know how to swim well; he can only _____ in the shallow end of the pool.

7. The king decided to _____ the evil man from the kingdom for the rest of his life.

8. The company has suffered one setback after another, and it seems to be _____ to failure.

1-26~31

Once upon a time in China, a man and his wife led a simple life of subsistence on their small plot of land. They had a ring which, unbeknown to them, was lucky.

5 Whoever had the ring would never be rich, but would always have enough to get by. As the man and his wife were unaware of this, they decided to sell the ring so that they might make

10 a bit of money. After they sold the ring, their fortunes fared worse and worse, and before long, they were poor and destitute.

The couple didn't have much on their small farm, but they did have a pair of
15 pets—a cat and a dog, to be precise. The cat and dog saw their masters suffering and wanted to do something for them. But what could they do? They thought about it for a while, and after a time the dog had an idea. They could go and steal the ring back, returning it to their masters and reversing their terrible fortune. The cat thought it was a wonderful idea. However, being
20 the realist of the pair, the cat pointed out that the ring was locked in a chest, which they couldn't open by themselves. The dog meditated on this for a time, too, and again came up with a plan. The dog
25 said that the cat could simply threaten a mouse into making a hole through the chest. Then the mouse could scurry inside and fetch the ring for them.

With the plan in place, the cat and
30 the dog set out across the countryside, bound for the house which now held the ring somewhere within its walls. On the way there, they came upon a raging river.

So fast was the current that the water boiled up in great, crashing waves that broke upon the banks. The cat was terrified because it couldn't swim. Luckily, the dog was a very strong swimmer. Taking up the cat by the collar with his teeth, he was able to paddle against the torrent, speeding them to safety on the opposite side. 35

After their ordeal at the river, the dog and the cat took a quick trip through farmers' fields and eventually reached the house where they could find the ring. Quietly, they sneaked inside, where they found a mouse scrounging for small pieces of bread in a corner. The mouse was terrified, facing down its mortal enemy. The cat said that they 40 would let the mouse live if the mouse would chew a hole through the chest that held the ring and retrieve it for them. Shaking with fear, the mouse agreed to the task.

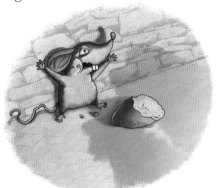

True to its word, the mouse stole the ring from the chest and brought it to the cat. Then, 45 the dog and the cat began their journey home, going back the same way they came. When they again reached the river, the dog had a better strategy. This time the cat rode on the dog's back across the deadly expanse, holding the ring 50 in its mouth. On reaching the other side, the soaking wet dog gave pause to shake the water from its fur. As it did, the cat excitedly burst forward, running for home. When the cat got home, it humbly presented the ring to the man and his wife. They

### Notes

**torrent** *n.* strong and fast moving water
**sneak** *v.* to move quietly and secretly
**scrounge** *v.* to get things from whatever source is available
**expanse** *n.* a wide continuous area of land, water, or sky
**humbly** *adv.* acting as if one is in a lower position

stood stunned in sight of their pet returning the source of their salvation. No more
55  would they have to scratch a meager living from the poor soil. Now, they would
always have what they needed to survive. Grateful, they promised to care for the cat
like a son for the rest of its days.

    As they finished making their solemn oath to the cat, the dog returned.
Thinking that the dog had not aided the cat on its quest to save the family, the man
60  and his wife were very angry. They banished the dog from the house, and the dog
was doomed to wander the countryside. As it did, the dog spread the tale of the
cat's betrayal to every fellow dog that passed by. Since then, dogs have never passed
up an opportunity to chase any cat that crosses their path.

## Notes

**stunned**  *adj.*  greatly surprised and astonished
**meager**  *adj.*  very small or limited

# Reading Comprehension

**Multiple Choice:** Based on the reading, choose the best answer to each question.

DETAIL     1. What would happen to those who possessed the ring mentioned in
              the story?

              a. They would have enough for ten lifetimes.

              b. They would have more than enough to get by.

              c. They would instantly become very rich.

              d. They would have enough to survive on.

DETAIL     2. Which of the following is NOT true?

              a. The dog was loyal to its masters.

              b. The dog suggested that they take the ring back.

              c. The cat wanted to help the masters, but the dog didn't.

              d. The cat threatened a mouse so that the mouse would help steal
                 the ring.

PHRASE     3. In Lines 39–40, the phrase "facing down" is closest in meaning to

              _____.

              a. running away from

              b. taking care of

              c. being confronted by

              d. being looked down on

DETAIL     4. What did the man and woman think about their pets when the cat
              and the dog came home?

              a. The dog had done all the work.

              b. The dog had not helped the cat.

              c. The cat had not gone on the journey at all.

              d. The cat had taken the ring from the dog.

INFERENCE  5. Why did the dog spread the tale of the cat's betrayal?

              a. The cat took all the credit for helping the masters.

              b. The cat killed the mouse that had obtained the ring for them.

              c. The masters decided to treat the mouse like a son.

              d. The masters let the cat wander the countryside.

GIST       6. Which of the following would make the best alternate title for this
              story?

              a. Cats and Dogs: Partners in Crime

              b. Cats and Dogs: The Oldest of Enemies

              c. Dogs and Cats: How to Train them to Get Along

              d. Dogs and Cats: A Tale of Enduring Friendship

**Think More**

1. What do you
   think is the
   purpose of most
   folk tales?

2. Do dogs really
   chase cats in
   real life? What
   may be the
   reason(s) for
   this?

# Reading Skill [ Identifying Character Traits ]

In a literary work, the author does not always directly describe the characters. So, as a reader, you have to build up your own knowledge about them. As you read, you can identify the character traits of a certain person or the personification of an animal by analyzing the words and the actions of the person or animal. Learning to identify character traits helps you understand the character's responses and emotions, and it also gives you some clue about how the story will proceed.

**Task 1:** Read through the short passage. Then, underline the words that tell you about Paul's character traits and write down some adjectives to describe Paul.

Paul works in the fashion industry. He doesn't really like his job, but he doesn't have the courage to make some changes. Besides, the salary is high, which has made it possible for him to own an apartment and a car. Although Paul knows many people in the fashion industry, he seldom goes out with them. He does not want to hang out with the same people he works with in his leisure time. Paul does not have a girlfriend now. A few years ago, he went out with a model, but the relationship ended in disaster. From then on, he has decided not to trust any woman.

I think Paul is _____.

**Task 2:** Read the second paragraph of Reading. Then, use some of the adjectives in the box to describe the dog and the cat. Some can be used more than once.

| loyal | persuasive | intelligent | doubtful | lazy | realistic | cowardly |
|---|---|---|---|---|---|---|

The dog: _____     The cat: _____

# Vocabulary Builder [ The Suffix -en ]

The suffix -en can be added to nouns or adjectives to form adjectives or verbs. When it is used to make a verb, it means "to make something have a certain quality." For example, in Reading, we saw the word *threaten*, which is a combination of *threat* and -en, meaning "to make a threat." When the suffix is used to make an adjective, it means "something is made of a certain material or looks like a certain material," for example, *golden*.

**Task 1:** Look at the following words. Write the correct parts of speech for them (V for verb and A for adjective) and match them to the correct definitions.

1. weaken (   )   •                    • made of clay
2. brighten (   )   •                   • make something lighter
3. wooden (   )   •                     • become longer
4. strengthen (   )   •                 • made of wood
5. earthen (   )   •                    • make someone or something less powerful
6. lengthen (   )   •                   • become stronger

**Task 2:** Use the words from the box to complete the passage. Change the word form if necessary.

| shorten | whiten | freshen | straighten |
|---------|--------|---------|------------|

Monica went to the spa to get a makeover. First, she wanted to do something with her teeth. The spa technician said he could (1)_____ them for her and make them shine. Next, Monica turned her attention to her hair. It was very long, and she wanted to (2)_____ it for a change. It was also very curly, and she wanted to (3)_____ it out. By the time she was finished, she really had (4)_____ up her look. She was very pleased with the results.

## Let's Think About It!

In this unit, we read a folk tale about why dogs chase cats. Folk tales usually have one thing in common. In a folksy way, they provide an explanation (however unlikely) for why a common phenomenon takes place. This phenomenon can be natural, behavioral, or anything else you might imagine.

In a group of four, come up with a folk tale of your own. First, take a look at the following phenomena. Then, choose one to use to develop your own folk tale. You can discuss this with your group members and talk about the title you want to give to your folk tale. Next, come up with the characters in your tale and outline a plot, which should include what is going to happen at the beginning, the middle, and the end. When you complete the tale, share it with the class.

| Phenomenon | Title | Character(s) | Plot Outline |
|-----------|-------|--------------|--------------|
| Why do sunflowers face toward the sun? | | | |
| Why is the sky blue? | | | |
| Why does a bat like to hang upside down? | | | |

# The Man Who Grew a Forest

## Let's Get Started

### A. Before You Read

1. Look at the following pictures and match them to the environmental terms below.

| Recycling | Renewable Energy | Reforestation | Power Conserving |

2. Do you make any efforts to be environmentally friendly? What kinds of things do you do? In which areas might you improve?

3. Do you know of any people or organizations who work to protect the environment? What do they do?

### B. Words in Context

🎧 1-32

Use the words from the box to complete the following sentences. Change the word form if necessary.

| | | | |
|---|---|---|---|
| curriculum | erosion | sprawling | deduce |
| array | grumble | barren | at one's disposal |

1. Much to Watson's surprise, Holmes quickly _____ that the killer must have been left-handed.

2. The coastline of the island has been retreating for years due to _____ from the sea.

3. I was amazed by the _____ of products available in Akihabara, the electronics district in Tokyo.

4. Protestors complained about the government's plan to build a(n) _____ department store on the land.

5. Australia's aborigines lived for thousands of years on _____ land where Europeans found it impossible to survive.

6. There is no point in _____ about the assignment. We just have to get on with it.

7. It was little wonder the team won the competition with all the talented players it has _____.

8. The school has decided to update its _____ in order to include courses in new types of technology, such as artificial intelligence.

There's a saying that someone who sees details but not the whole situation "can't see the forest for the trees." Jadav Payeng never had this problem. As a 16-year-old, he had a life-changing experience. Wandering along the river banks of the Brahmaputra, one of the world's mightiest rivers, he came across hundreds of
5   dead snakes washed up on the shore. Being a perceptive young man, Payeng quickly deduced how the creatures had met their fate: death from excessive heat due to a lack of shelter.

The year was 1979, and Payeng's home state of Assam in northern India was in the midst of the annual monsoon season, which ravages the region and causes
10  severe flooding. For years, deforestation had been a problem in the region, and the consequences were now plain to see. With the loss of trees, the floods caused erosion of the top soil—the part of the earth that carries the nutrients required to sustain plant life. Furthermore, when vegetation cannot grow properly, a cycle of destruction occurs, as the roots of trees
15  and plants help to keep the soil in place. In hilly and mountainous areas, the results can be disastrous. Simply put, no trees equals more landslides, and these can wipe out entire villages.

20  Back to the unfortunate reptiles. Payeng realized that the disappearance of forests around the Brahmaputra was affecting the region's animal life in more ways than one. Local villagers, for
25  example, noted the disappearance of many species of birds that were finding nesting sites increasingly scarce. They pointed out the connections that might not have been obvious to
30  outsiders. Fewer birds meant fewer

Jadav Payeng

Jadav Payeng grew a forest starting from 20 bamboo seedlings.

eggs and chicks, which are a source of food for snakes and other predators. Village elders encouraged Payeng to do what he could to help, furnishing him with around 20 bamboo seedlings to plant. They chose bamboo as it is a hardy plant that grows quickly and requires little in the way of nutrients. Selecting the island of Mājuli—the world's largest river island—Payeng set to work.                                       35

Soon after he had planted these first seedlings, Payeng began working for the local forestry division on a project to develop the barren areas of the island. This project lasted almost five years and provided around 200 hectares of forest. However, Payeng is not one to do things by halves, and he stuck around for quite a while after the conclusion of the project. In fact, he has continued to plant trees      40 and plants on the island every single day for over 35 years and counting.

Payeng had to overcome various difficulties, most notably in creating an irrigation system for his growing forest. Although he had an enormous water source at his disposal, there was no way one man could use it to tend to such a large area of land. To get around this obstacle, Payeng constructed a series of bamboo      45 platforms over each plant. On each of these wooden shelves stood clay pots with tiny holes in them. These released water drop by drop, slowly watering the plants below over the course of a week. To improve the fertility of the soil, Payeng introduced earthworms, ants, and termites. Ants help break down rocky soil, and termites release a chemical that improves soil quality, both of which make it easier      50 to grow things.

## Notes

**chick**  *n.*  a baby bird
**seedling**  *n.*  a young plant that has grown from a seed
**earthworm**  *n.*  a long, thin creature that lives in soil
**termite**  *n.*  a small insect that usually feeds on wood

Incredibly, what began as a few bamboo seedlings has now grown into a sprawling 550-acre jungle. Keen to ensure the forest did not end up the same way as the trees that had previously occupied the island, Payeng planted only low-value plants for the first 20 years or so. However, from the late 1980s onwards, he began to add larger, sturdier trees. As he had hoped, the forest soon attracted an array of wild animals. Tigers, rhinos, and deer now roam freely among the greenery that Payeng nurtured with his own hands.

Of course, the forest requires protection from poachers, and Payeng pays daily trips to check that all is well. Urban commuters grumbling about their commute to work each day should consider Payeng's daily routine. Up at 3 a.m., he cycles for an hour to reach the river, then rows five kilometers to the island. After that, he cycles for another 30 minutes to reach the field where he keeps cattle. After he has milked his cows, an activity that helps him support his family, he visits the forest. Despite his best efforts, animals have been killed. The death of a rhino, killed for its horn in 2012, deeply upset him, and he has strongly criticized the local government for not assisting with conservation efforts. Yet, he admits that no amount of legal protection can put a stop to illegal hunting and deforestation. The answer, he firmly believes, lies in education. "Planting of trees should be part of the school curriculum," Payeng says. "Each child should plant two trees and look after them till they leave school."

Jadav Payeng in his forest

Payeng does not see himself as an educator or public figure, preferring instead to focus on his work. However, he has agreed to speak at schools and international conferences both in India and abroad. An ability to see the bigger picture best sums Jadav Payeng up. He is a man who both figuratively and literally was able to see both the trees and the forest that they became.

## Notes

**sturdy** *adj.* strong, solid, or durable
**rhino** *n.* short form of rhinoceros, a large, heavy animal with armored skin and one or two horns on its nose
**roam** *v.* to wander or move from place to place with no plan or purpose
**poacher** *n.* a person who hunts animals illegally
**figuratively** *adv.* in a way that uses words and phrases with an imaginative meaning

# Reading Comprehension

**Multiple Choice:** Based on the reading, choose the best answer to each question.

CONTEXT 1. What does the term "nesting sites" in Line 27 refer to?

    a. Sources to find nutrients

    b. Places to build homes

    c. Shelters from hot weather

    d. Rivers to locate water

PARAPHRASE 2. What does the author mean by "Payeng is not one to do things by halves" in Line 39?

    a. He is always on time.

    b. He is very balanced.

    c. He works longer than others.

    d. He always gives his best effort.

INFERENCE 3. What was the enormous resource at Payeng's disposal?

    a. The Brahmaputra

    b. The forest

    c. The island

    d. The local elders

INFERENCE 4. What does the author imply about Payeng's decision to plant low-value trees?

    a. It started in the late 1980s.

    b. It stopped people from cutting down trees.

    c. It provided better shelter for wild animals.

    d. It turned out to be a mistake.

DETAIL 5. How does Payeng earn a living?

    a. By planting trees

    b. By protecting animals

    c. By selling milk

    d. By catching poachers

DETAIL 6. What is NOT something Payeng has done to protect the forest?

    a. Become involved in education

    b. Design an irrigation system

    c. Breed cattle

    d. Release insects

## Think More

1. Do you think the efforts of people like Jadav Payeng will be enough to solve environmental problems? If not, what else must be done?

2. Some politicians and public officials claim that there is no proof that global warming is caused by humans. Why might they say this?

# Reading Skill — Guessing the Meaning of Unfamiliar Vocabulary

Reading texts may contain words or phrases with which we are unfamiliar. Besides using context clues as demonstrated in the previous unit, the meaning of an unknown word might be guessed from its prefix, suffix, or root word. Often, a combination of factors might give us a good clue to the meaning of a word or phrase.

**Task 1:** Look at the paragraph and then answer the following question. Give the reason(s) for your answer.

The Organization for Economic Cooperation and Development has warned that global economic growth may be affected by countries that pursue <u>protectionism</u>. In its latest economic outlook report, the OECD noted that nations that excessively tax imports to shield domestic industries may be contributing to economic slowdown.

The word "protectionism" is closest in meaning to a policy that _____.
a. slows down global economic growth
b. raises excessive taxes on a country's citizens
c. protects a country's own industries
d. protects a country's citizens from violence

Reason(s): _____

**Task 2:** Read the second paragraph of Reading. As you read, find the words that match the definitions below and write them in the spaces provided.

1. the removal of trees → _____

2. to keep something existing → _____

3. trees and plants → _____

# Vocabulary Builder — The Suffixes -ery and -ry

The suffix -ery and the shortened form -ry are used in various ways. In Reading, for example, we saw the words *forestry* and *greenery*. The first word refers to the occupation of working to maintain forests, and the second refers to plants and vegetation. There are several general ways of categorizing words that use these suffixes.

**Task 1:** Classify the words in the box according to the general rules in the table below. The first one has been done for you.

machinery   winery   slavery   artistry   jewelry   ~~greenery~~   dentistry   brewery   bakery

| Things in a group or collection | An occupation or condition | A place where something is done |
|---|---|---|
| greenery | | |

**Task 2:** Choose a word from Task 1 to complete the sentences.

1. We were allowed to sample some of the different beers during our visit to the
   _____.

2. Michelangelo was famed for his _____ in a number of fields.

3. Do not operate this _____ when you are tired, as it could be dangerous.

## Let's Think About It!

As environmental awareness increases, more and more eco-friendly products are being produced. These might use recyclable materials or manufacturing processes that don't harm the environment. They might also help to conserve energy. Work in groups of four and come up with an innovative green product. Then, hold a short press conference or product launch to introduce it. An example has been done for you in the table below.

| Type of Product | Brand Name | Features | Target Market | Cost |
|---|---|---|---|---|
| Self-powering computer | Taptronic | Keyboard that converts typing into energy | Young professionals | US$2,000 |
| | | | | |
| | | | | |

# Find Your Dream Job Today

# Let's Get Started

## A. Before You Read

1. Which of the following aspects do you consider important for a dream job? Check the ones that are important to you.

☐ high pay    ☐ challenging    ☐ nice coworkers    ☐ rewarding

☐ an encouraging boss    ☐ good benefits    ☐ close to home

☐ potential for advancement    ☐ a chance to help society

2. With a partner, discuss why you chose these aspects. Then, share with your partner what job or what type of work you would like to do in the future.

## B. Words in Context

CD 1-41

Use the words from the box to complete the following sentences. Change the word form if necessary.

| | | | |
|---|---|---|---|
| seminar | aspiration | gloomy | revelation |
| questionnaire | vocation | minimal | virtual |

1. At the _____, an expert on cybercrime presented several cases of online credit card fraud.

2. I was surprised by Tom's _____ that he is very unhappy at his current job.

3. By using our _____ campus, you can attend classes without actually having to set foot on university grounds.

4. It's not surprising that Sally has a(n) _____ look on her face on this rainy Monday morning.

5. Since you are patient and like to help others, being a teacher would be an ideal _____ for you.

6. If you want to help other people, then you have to understand their needs and _____.

7. If you think getting in shape will require _____ effort, think again.

8. Please fill out this _____; your answers are very important to our research.

1-42~47

Do you find yourself stuck in a rut career-wise? Are you often overcome with feelings of dread and anxiety at the mere thought of going to work? And when you finally do get to work, do you find yourself whiling away the hours, just staring at the clock, pining for the day to be over? If you answered yes to one or more of these
5    questions, chances are you've not yet found your ideal vocation or place of employment. Luckily, we at Caves Career Institute are here to help.

At Caves Career Institute, our team of career experts is standing by to advise you on all matters related to career development for those fresh out of college or university, just starting out in the working world, or for industry veterans looking
10    to get the most out of their remaining years. Our initial session with you starts with one fundamental question: Is your current job what you always dreamed of doing? More often than not, the answer is a gloomy "no." But don't despair just yet. This revelation is just the first step on your path toward doing what your heart desires.

15    From this initial question, the real work begins. It isn't always easy to determine your ideal profession, but it is always worthwhile to find out what it is. Sometimes, in order to unlock your innermost desires and dreams, it requires more than just filling out a simple questionnaire, which is as deep as many
20    of our competitors delve. At Caves Career Institute, we employ a dedicated team of psychiatrists who, over the course of several sessions, will spend time with you, peeling back the layers
25    of your subconscious to reveal those wants and needs which may have been covered by years of neglect. These experts are helpful in leading our clients back to a simpler time in their
30    lives—a time when their dreams and aspirations for the future were

## Notes

**stuck in a rut** *idiom* being unable to change the repetitive pattern of one's life
**innermost** *adj.* of thoughts or feelings that are most private and personal
**delve** *v.* to research or dig into something
**psychiatrist** *n.* a doctor who treats patients with a mental illness

A career development course

foremost in their minds, before the distractions of life came into play. Oftentimes, our clients who have completed these sessions will gain a sense of clarity in regard to their career that they never thought possible.

Following the psychiatric sessions, our clients move on to the next phase in     35
our career development course. These involve classes and seminars with our
award-winning team of life coaches and motivational speakers. In spending time
with these inspirational people, all of whom have overcome great odds to achieve
high levels of success in their chosen fields, our clients will learn to pursue their life
goals and attain the required career skills in a systematic way. Those leading the     40
classes and seminars include former professional athletes, captains of industry, and
men and women who dared to do the impossible. For a full list of instructors and
speakers, please log on to our website at cavescareerinstitute.com.

Our services don't just end with classes and seminars. After completing our
program, our clients are provided with abundant opportunities to intern at their     45

## Notes

**distraction**  *n.*  something that takes your attention away from something else
**oftentimes**  *adv.*  often
**clarity**  *n.*  the condition of being clear
**odds**  *n. (pl.)*  difficulties

People in all walks of life

desired company or in a certain career field. In addition, as they move on with their working lives, they are free to return for follow-up sessions with our staff for a minimal fee. Sometimes they come back to receive more career advice, and sometimes they just come back for an extra dose of motivation. No matter what
50    they might require, Caves Career Institute is here to make sure they don't lose sight of their career goals and keep going after the job that is meaningful to them.

To enroll at Caves Career Institute, simply fill out our online application form. On our website, you can also take a virtual tour of our premises and watch introductory videos from our staff. If you would like to come by for an in-person
55    tour of Caves Career Institute, simply call ahead or send us an email to make the arrangements. Enrollment is always open, and your sessions can begin whenever you are ready to discover your true passion and gain a sense of fulfillment. Contact Caves Career Institute today!

## Note

**fulfillment**  *n.*  achievment of one's ambitions or desires

# Reading Comprehension

**Multiple Choice:** Based on the reading, choose the best answer to each question.

PURPOSE   1. What is the main purpose of this article?

     a. To advertise a school wherein students can graduate with high scores

     b. To explain the content of a questionnaire related to jobs

     c. To offer free assistance in getting one's career off the ground

     d. To promote a service related to career development

VOCABULARY   2. What does the word "veterans" in Line 9 most likely mean?

     a. People who are experienced in the workforce

     b. People who want to find their true passion

     c. Career experts at Caves Career Institute

     d. University or college graduates

INFERENCE   3. What does the article imply about Caves Career Institute's competitors?

     a. They offer services very similar to those at Caves Career Institute.

     b. They merely have their attendees fill out a questionnaire.

     c. They have services far beyond those offered by the institute.

     d. They offer the same services but are much more expensive.

DETAIL   4. What do the life coaches and speakers at Caves Career Institute all have in common?

     a. They all have a background in psychiatry.

     b. They were all once professional athletes.

     c. They are all successful in their careers.

     d. They can all provide internship opportunities.

DETAIL   5. How can people enroll at Caves Career Institute?

     a. They just need to fill out a form online.

     b. They must do so in person at the institute.

     c. They should either call in or send an e-mail.

     d. They must go through a series of tests first.

GIST   6. Who does this article target?

     a. Those who are aiming for an early retirement

     b. Those who are looking for a better salary

     c. Those who wish to become captains of industry

     d. Those who have not yet attained their ideal job

**Think More**

1. What is your dream job? What skills or qualities do you need in order to get it?

2. Do you think it is necessary for everyone to find a dream job? Why or why not?

## Reading Skill — Recognizing an Author's Motivation

Every piece of writing has a purpose. So, it's important for readers to be able to ascertain why the author wrote an article in order to gain a general understanding of it. The author's motivation can be revealed by the overall tone of the article, the facts presented within the article, and which side of an issue the author tends to lean toward.

**Task 1:** Below is the opening paragraph of an article. Scan it quickly and answer the following questions.

Cancer is becoming increasingly prevalent today owing to many factors, such as changes to the human diet, exposure to UV radiation, and chemicals present in food products and other objects we use on a daily basis. There was a time when cancer was a death sentence for most people. Thanks to advances in biotechnology, however, the rate of curing the disease is on the rise. Now, B.P Pharma, one of the most renowned biopharmaceutical companies in Europe, is unveiling a new gene therapy program that could possibly treat cancer patients in a more effective way.

1. What may be the purpose of this article?
   a. To persuade people to eat less foods with chemicals
   b. To name some of the reasons why cancer is more common today
   c. To introduce a new kind of treatment for cancer

2. What is the overall tone of this paragraph?
   a. Depressing                    b. Humorous                    c. Hopeful

**Task 2:** Read the first paragraph of Reading. What seems to be the author's motivation for writing the article?

The author wrote this article in order to _____

_____.

## Vocabulary Builder — The Prefix *sub-*

The prefix *sub-* is usually attached to words to give the meaning of "under, below, beneath, or smaller." In Reading, we saw the word *subconscious*. This literally means "below the conscious mind," and it refers to the part of the mind that contains unnoticeable thoughts. Other words with the prefix *sub-* include *subway*, *submarine*, and *subculture*.

**Task 1:** Which of the following words can take the prefix *sub-*? Write the prefix in the space for those which can take it or put an "X" in front of the words which can't.

1. _____market                          2. _____committee

3. _____plot                            4. _____text

5. _____pass                            6. _____tropical

7. _____standard                        8. _____shore

**Task 2:** Use the words with the prefix *sub-* from Task 1 to complete the passage.

I've been reading a novel recently. The story takes place on a (1)_____ island. The main plot revolves around a team of researchers who are sent to the island to investigate sightings of ancient creatures thought to be long extinct. In the (2)_____, the book delves into the personal relationships between the main characters as the island throws all types of challenges at them. The (3)_____ within the story is the theme of human beings' desire to control nature. However, so far I think the book is (4)_____. It lacks excitement and a single, unifying voice. Sometimes when I am reading this book, I feel as if I am listening to some sort of (5)_____ trying to preach to me. I hope that it will get better soon.

## Let's Think About It!

There are many new and exciting jobs nowadays that people might have never thought about doing before. In a group of four to six, tell the other members of the group what your dream job might be. First, write down your dream job in the chart below and some related information about it. You can even create a new job that nobody has ever heard of! Then, share your answers with your partners. Remember, the more unconventional the job is, the more fun it will be!

| | | |
|---|---|---|
| **My Dream Job** | eSports player | |
| **Required Skills** | • Exceptional video gaming skills<br>• Great observation skills<br>• Having quick reactions | |
| **Ideal Personality Traits** | • Passionate<br>• Competitive | |
| **Advantages** | • High salary<br>• Exciting and fun | |
| **Disadvantages** | • Very hard to become professional<br>• Harmful to the eyes | |
| **Other(s)** | | |

# Review 1 (Units 1–6)

## I. Definition Matching

*Match the words to the correct definitions.*

1. consciousness •          • to send away and prevent from returning

2. counterpart •          • one's awareness or perception of something

3. compile •          • feeling unhappy and hopeless

4. banish •          • another person or thing with a similar position or function

5. gloomy •          • to produce or make something by assembling information, songs, etc.

## II. Sentence Completion

*Choose the correct words to complete the sentences.*

1. Where can I download those cute animal stickers you have for LINE? They are absolutely
   _____.
   a. adorable          b. collective          c. inappropriate          d. obsessed

2. This _____ species of snake can only be found on one very small South Pacific island.
   a. exotic          b. humid          c. collective          d. ordinary

3. Statistics show that the global _____, or the total number of people in employment, is somewhere around three billion people.
   a. awareness          b. consequence          c. workforce          d. aisle

4. Paul wrote to his favorite author in the hope that she would write the _____ to his new book.
   a. foresight          b. forearm          c. foreword          d. forecast

5. In the famous video game, Super Mario goes on a _____ to save Princess Peach.
   a. vacation          b. betrayal          c. quest          d. habitat

6. Ian was on a bad path in life before he discovered basketball, which he thinks of as his _____.
   a. oath          b. salvation          c. betrayal          d. scarf

7. The ruins of the ancient city contained an advanced _____ system for agriculture.
   a. irrigation          b. erosion          c. cohabitation          d. innovation

8. Ken has originally planned to become a doctor, but in the end he chose _____ as his profession.
   a. winery          b. dentistry          c. greenery          d. slavery

9. Being a musician isn't just a job for Charles, it's his ideal _____.
   a. sensation          b. vocation          c. revelation          d. distraction

10. Mandy has always had a(n) _____ to become a famous actress on Broadway.
    a. seminar          b. aspiration          c. collar          d. rut

## III. Cloze Test

*Choose the correct words to complete the passages.*

**A**

When my friends heard that I wanted to open a themed bookstore about dogs, they thought I was crazy. They knew I was __1__ with little animals and that I loved reading. However, they didn't think I could make money by combining these two interests. I __2__ why they felt shocked, but opening a themed bookstore is __3__ a trend. More and more people keep dogs nowadays, and they enjoy their furry friends' __4__. So, from the perspective of these dog owners, it is beneficial to have a dog-themed bookstore which provides them with professional books about dog health, training, and even psychology. I have no __5__ that these dog owners would want to know more about their pets.

1. a. obsessed        b. celebrated        c. adorable        d. collective

2. a. threaten        b. paddle        c. comprehend        d. destitute

3. a. considerably        b. accordingly        c. definitely        d. occasionally

4. a. opportunity        b. companionship        c. curriculum        d. mammal

5. a. trend        b. plot        c. outcome        d. doubt

**B**

If you're an unsigned musician, you probably can't count on digital formats to sell your music. Streaming services like Spotify give low payments to musicians. __1__, with the number of artists on Spotify right now passing the eight million __2__, it can be difficult to stand out. However, streaming services have their advantages because they make your music __3__ to the public. As a worst-case scenario, your songs won't get many plays, but the only thing you've lost is a small amount of time putting up your songs, which is really just a minor __4__. That's why more and more musicians are choosing to put their music on Spotify every day, with many more ready to __5__.

1. a. Otherwise        b. However        c. Besides        d. Nevertheless

2. a. observer        b. mark        c. server        d. spark

3. a. indefensible        b. incapable        c. unbreakable        d. accessible

4. a. setback        b. guilt        c. beta        d. heap

5. a. pack up        b. drop out        c. follow suit        d. cash in on

## IV. Reading Comprehension

*Read the articles and choose the correct answers.*

Men and women seem to be getting married later and later nowadays, and there is statistical proof of this phenomenon in countries such as the US, Canada, Japan, etc. In many of these places, politicians, and indeed society at large, are reacting with shock and alarm, but often with good reason.

In places like Japan, it won't be long before the majority of the population is elderly. As more and more young people are delaying marriage, the country's birth rate is plummeting as the average age climbs ever higher. This means a smaller workforce and fewer young people to pay into the social welfare systems that care for the elderly.

This could have huge consequences for what is still currently one of the world's strongest economies. In fact, all strong economies require a steady supply of workers to pay into those systems which provide care for the old, the sick, and the otherwise **infirm**. Marriage usually plays a role in that, either directly or indirectly. Marriage, more often than not, means children. With rising costs in many countries and an increasingly bleak view of the institution of marriage in general on the rise in the Information Age, even married couples are increasingly choosing not to have kids. So, we can see how delaying marriage can sometimes lead to a falling population and the subsequent economic pitfalls therein.

What can governments do to prevent this? They might offer marriage incentives. In Canada, for example, married couples enjoy tax benefits, and they can apply for subsidies when they have kids. Other governments around the world facing problems associated with delayed marriage and population decline might think about following suit.

1. What is the main purpose of this article?
   a. To show that marriage is not a requirement in modern times
   b. To prove that getting married earlier in life is better than waiting
   c. To talk about the benefits of delaying marriage
   d. To discuss the various impacts of people delaying marriage

2. When most people seem to delay marriage, what is the reaction from politicians?
   a. They are in favor of it.
   b. They are concerned about it.
   c. They have no strong reaction to it.
   d. They are ambivalent toward it.

3. The word "infirm" in the third paragraph is closest in meaning to _____.
   a. lazy   b. unhappy   c. unhealthy   d. rich

4. Which of the following can be inferred from the article?
   a. The longer people wait to get married, the better off a nation will be financially.
   b. The more elderly there are in a country, the better off the economy will be.
   c. A weak institution of marriage, overall, means a healthier economy.
   d. A strong institution of marriage can be linked to a strong economy.

5. How does delaying marriage affect the economy, according to the article?
   a. It equals more kids, which equals more mouths to feed.
   b. It equals fewer elderly, which means less economic burden.
   c. It means fewer children, which leads to a smaller workforce.
   d. It means more children, which leads to a stronger economy.

The story of why cats and dogs are mortal enemies is, as most people would consider, just a story. But some animal myths are actually rooted in scientific fact. One of those myths is also an old proverb: An elephant never forgets. Is this really true, or just another tall tale passed on from one generation to the next?

The phrase "an elephant never forgets" likely started when biologists realized that elephants have the largest brain of any land animal. It was fairly common for people at that time to think that the bigger the brain, the better the memory. In fact, it's true in some ways. Elephants are territorial, and they have a huge home range. An elephant's home territory can be over 3,000 square kilometers. That's about the same size as the relatively small American state of Rhode Island. But research has shown that elephants can remember their entire territory, much in the same way humans retain a memory of the familiar area in which they grew up.

Family is important to elephants, too. They travel in family-based herds, staying together for years. As is the case with humans, though, when things get a little too crowded, it's time for one of the kids to move out. The one who moves out, when it comes to elephants, is the eldest daughter. She breaks off and starts her own herd. But she never forgets her family. One researcher found that a female was still able to recognize her mother, even after the two of them had been separated for 23 years. So, it seems that the old adage about an elephant's memory definitely holds true.

1. What does the article imply about animal myths?
   a. Some are just stories, but some are actually true.
   b. Animal myths can sometimes be misleading.
   c. Animal myths about cats and dogs are usually just stories.
   d. Proverbs can prove them true.

2. What can we infer from the article about the character traits of elephants?
   a. They can't travel in groups.
   b. They are aggressive.
   c. They are heavy creatures.
   d. They are family-oriented.

3. What is true of an elephant's home range, according to the article?
   a. It is as big as a medium-sized nation.
   b. It is the same size as a small state.
   c. It is about the same size as a small town.
   d. It is lesser in size than a few city blocks.

4. When a herd of elephants gets too big, which elephant will leave?
   a. The oldest male
   b. The oldest male child
   c. The oldest female
   d. The oldest female child

5. What has research shown about elephants when it comes to family members?
   a. They will gradually forget family members after moving out.
   b. They will reunite with one another 23 years later.
   c. They can remember one another even after decades apart.
   d. They can remember the directions to their homes.

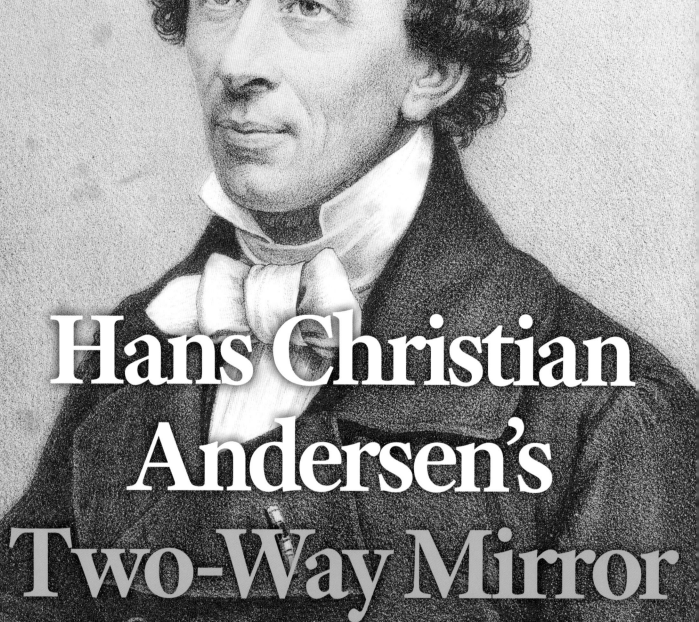

# Hans Christian Andersen's Two-Way Mirror

# Let's Get Started

## A. Before You Read

**1.** Match the photos to the different types of books.

| textbook | novel | autobiography | reference book |

**2.** Did you have a favorite author or type of book when you were younger? Why did you like that writer or style?

## B. Words in Context

 2-01

Use the words from the box to complete the following sentences. Change the word form if necessary.

| anticipate | celebrated | insecure | mimic |
|---|---|---|---|
| conspicuous | feminine | exclaim | scorn |

**1.** Adam does not like speaking in public as he feels _____ about his voice.

**2.** On seeing the advertisement for the new movie, the boy _____ that it looked fantastic.

**3.** The claim that evolution is unproven has been received with _____ by many scientists.

**4.** As weird at it may sound, the recent strange events in my life seem to be _____ the events in the famous movie.

**5.** We _____ a continued increase in sales over the next two quarters.

**6.** When travelling in countries where robbery is common, it's a good idea to wear clothing that doesn't look _____.

**7.** Yoga was once regarded by many as a(n) _____ exercise, but that is no longer the case as more and more men start to practice it.

**8.** We were glad that we had the chance to listen to the speech by the _____ author.

2-02~09

"Life imitates art far more than art imitates life," wrote Oscar Wilde. The celebrated Irish writer was disputing the accepted view that artists depict the reality around them. Instead, he was convinced that events in the real world took their cue from creative works. Sometimes, the process seems to work both ways.

5    The life and work of Hans Christian Andersen are a case in point. Famed for his fairy tales, Andersen is one of the most renowned and beloved storytellers of all time. Yet, he suffered incredible heartache and sadness throughout his life. Many of his stories featured characters who were social outcasts. These lonely, awkward figures would suffer the scorn of society as they struggled to make sense of the
10   cruel circumstances in which they found themselves.

Perhaps the most famous example is *The Ugly Duckling*. This is the story of a small, shy baby duck who is laughed at and bullied because of his unattractive appearance. Unknown to the duckling and the other ducks, he was actually hatched from a swan's egg that accidentally rolled into a duck's nest. Eventually, he grows
15   into a beautiful, graceful swan who is praised for his good looks. Since its publication in 1843, this tale has served as a confidence booster for insecure youngsters the world over.

20   It is unsurprising that Anderson was able to write stories that young people could so readily identify with. As a young man, he was
25   painfully self-conscious about his appearance. He was tall, long-limbed, and had a nose that was conspicuous by its length. As he grew, he

Statue of Andersen and the ugly duckling in Central Park, New York

## Notes

**famed** *adj.* being widely known and admired
**heartache** *n.* great sadness and emotional pain
**outcast** *n.* a person who is rejected by society or a group
**booster** *n.* something that increases a positive quality or thing
**long-limbed** *adj.* having long arms and legs

Andersen's fairy tales in a bookstore

Hans Christian Andersen

developed a passion for singing and theater, which were considered feminine 30
pursuits. Coupled with his odd looks, this led to him being "cruelly teased and
mocked by other children," according to one biographer. Yet, like the ugly duckling,
he was to rise above the bullies and ascend to beauty through his work. When a
critic later asked him whether he would write his autobiography, Andersen replied
that he had already written it. He cited his best-known work as "a reflection of my 35
own life."

Born into a rural Danish community in 1805, Andersen was an only child,
and had a lonely upbringing. His family was far from rich, and it is no coincidence
that some of his most popular tales deal with themes of wealth and poverty. In *The
Little Match Girl*, for example, Andersen depicts the life of a poor young girl who is 40
left to freeze to death on the street. She is shunned by a society that seems to have
no pity.

Another of Andersen's renowned tales, *The Emperor's New Clothes*, is a world
away from this scene of urban poverty. Here, Andersen mocks wealthy people who
lack common sense. The story portrays a powerful ruler who is sold a suit of clothes 45
by tailors who say it is invisible only to idiots or people who cannot do their jobs
properly. Naturally, the emperor and his court do not want to be considered either
of these things, so they claim they can see the "clothes" perfectly. In the end, a child
puts an end to this ridiculous situation by exclaiming, "But he isn't wearing
anything at all!" According to some accounts, Andersen based this ending on a 50
childhood experience of seeing the Danish king. Surrounded by adults who were
treating the monarch as if he were divine, the young Andersen is said to have

## Notes

**cruelly**  *adv.*  in a way that causes pain or suffering to others
**ascend**  *v.*  to move in an upward direction
**upbringing**  *n.*  the way a person is raised or the things he or she is taught by his or her parents
**shun**  *v.*  to avoid or ignore

Hans Christian Andersen Fairy Tale House in Denmark

remarked, "Oh, he is nothing more than a human being!"

Throughout his life, Andersen had no luck in matters of the heart. He fell in
55    love with several women, and also at least one man, but his feelings were never
reciprocated. When he died in 1875, a letter from the first girl he had loved decades
earlier was found on his body. Yet, one woman stood out in his affections. This was
the Swedish singer Jenny Lind, who was the inspiration for *The Nightingale*. In this
tale, a Chinese emperor begins to tire of the beautiful singing of his favorite bird.
60    Instead, he starts to listen to a mechanical bird that has been given to him. When
he falls ill and is close to death, he desires to hear his nightingale singing again. The
bird returns and sings so sweetly that it saves the emperor's life.

Sadly for Andersen, there was to be no happy ending with the object of his
desires. However, Lind was very fond of the author, telling him she saw him as a
65    brother. In some senses, though, the details of *The Nightingale* did come true. For,
thanks to Andersen's story, Lind was soon to be known by the nickname "The
Swedish Nightingale." Life also seemed to mimic fiction in her relationship with a
man she really did love—the composer Fryderyk Chopin. During the serious illness
that was eventually to kill him, Chopin told Lind that her singing eased his pain.
70    Andersen's work had anticipated future events in a strange way that the author
could never have foreseen.

## Note

**reciprocate**   *v.*  to respond to an action or feeling with a similar action or feeling

**Multiple Choice:** Based on the reading, choose the best answer to each question.

INFERENCE   **1.** In Line 4, the expression "the process seems to work both ways" means _____.

    a. life imitates art and art imitates life

    b. creative people make creative things

    c. reality produces art more than artists reflect reality

    d. Oscar Wilde disputed accepted theories

INFERENCE   **2.** What did Andersen mean when he said that he had already written his autobiography?

    a. His life and upbringing was his autobiography.

    b. *The Ugly Duckling* was his autobiography.

    c. He did not want to reveal his life story.

    d. The facts of his life would be published after his death.

DETAIL   **3.** What is true of Andersen's family?

    a. They were wealthy.

    b. They lived far from rural areas.

    c. They did not have much money.

    d. They were ignored by society.

REFERENCE   **4.** In Lines 47–48, "either of these things" refers to _____.

    a. tailors and invisible things

    b. wealthy people and common sense

    c. powerful rulers and suits of clothes

    d. idiots and people who can't do their jobs well

DETAIL   **5.** Which of Andersen's tales supports Oscar Wilde's view?

    a. *The Ugly Duckling*

    b. *The Little Match Girl*

    c. *The Emperor's New Clothes*

    d. *The Nightingale*

GIST   **6.** What might the "two-way mirror" in the title of this unit refer to?

    a. Andersen's appearance

    b. Andersen's stories

    c. Andersen's life

    d. Andersen and those he loved

**Think More**

1. Do you know of any artists whose lives might have influenced their work? In what way?

2. Can you think of any examples of life imitating art?

Options or multiple choice questions may be designed to mislead you. For example, an option may include a statement that is true but which is not mentioned in the text. Another trick to watch out for is an option that uses words or phrases from the text to give an incorrect answer. Remember, just because an option contains key words from the text, it doesn't make it the right choice!

**Task 1:** Read the following passage and answer the question. Why is the answer incorrect?

There are several reasons why Joseph Conrad is counted among the greatest novelists in the English language. Firstly, he combined elements of two styles, realism and modernism, making him a bridge between the important authors of the late 19th and early 20th centuries. Furthermore, his innovative narrative style and use of the antihero influenced many other famous writers. Conrad's success is all the more impressive when one considers that he didn't become fluent in English until he was in his 20s.

Which of the following is NOT given as a reason for Conrad being a great novelist?
a. He mixed different writing styles.         b. He was not fluent in English.
c. He used a new narrative style.            d. His work featured antiheroes.

Explanation: _____

**Task 2:** Look at the fourth paragraph of Reading and answer the question below. Why are the other answers incorrect?

Why was Andersen teased as a child?
a. Because he looked like a girl           b. Because he was passionate
c. Because he had a long nose              d. Because he identified with young people

Explanation: _____

_____

_____

## Vocabulary Builder   Diminutive Suffixes

English contains a great number of suffixes known as diminutives. These are suffixes that suggest someone or something is smaller or younger than the original noun or a part of the noun. In Reading, we can see the word *duckling*, which used the suffix *-ling*. Other diminutive suffixes include *-ette* and *-let*.

**Task 1:** Which suffix do the following root words take? Add the correct diminutive suffix to the root words from the box and put them in the correct columns. The first one has been done for you.

| under | ~~kitchen~~ | cigar | drop | fledge | novel | book |

**-ette**

*kitchenette*

**-let**

**-ling**

**Task 2:** Choose a word from Task 1 to complete the following sentences.

1. A(n) _____ is a person of lower rank in a workplace.

2. A(n) _____ is the smallest amount of rain.

3. A(n) _____ is a young bird or an inexperienced person or thing.

## Let's Think About It!

In almost every field of the arts, there are awards for outstanding achievement. There are the Oscars for movies and the Grammys for music. There are also the Hans Christian Andersen Awards, which honor great authors and illustrators of children's literature every two years. But what if people were awarded prizes for everyday activities that they are usually not honored for? Work in teams of four to six and come up with prizes for people who you think are good at something, but who do not usually win a prize for this. Write some short award and acceptance speeches, and then practice them together. Remember: No "achievement" is too small!

| Name of Award Ceremony | *King of the Noodle Eaters* | |
|---|---|---|

### A. Award Speech

| Intro | Tonight's prize goes to a person who we feel has set a new standard when it comes to noodle eating. We are sure… | |
|---|---|---|
| Background (examples of achievements in the field) | On one particular occasion, we recall him eating two whole bowls of noodles in about five minutes! Everyone was amazed at his ability. Another time… | |
| Conclusion | In summing up, we would like to congratulate him on his achievement and present him with his prize—a lifetime's supply of noodles! The winner of this year's King of the Noodle Eaters goes to… | |

### B. Acceptance Speech

| Thanks | Thank you so much, everyone. It is my great honor to accept this prize. Firstly, I would like to… | |
|---|---|---|
| Background (how you managed to achieve this award) | It took many years of practice for me to get to this level of noodle eating. One method that I used was… | |
| Conclusion | Once again, I would like to thank everyone who helped me, and I hope to continue improving my noodle-eating skills in the future… | |

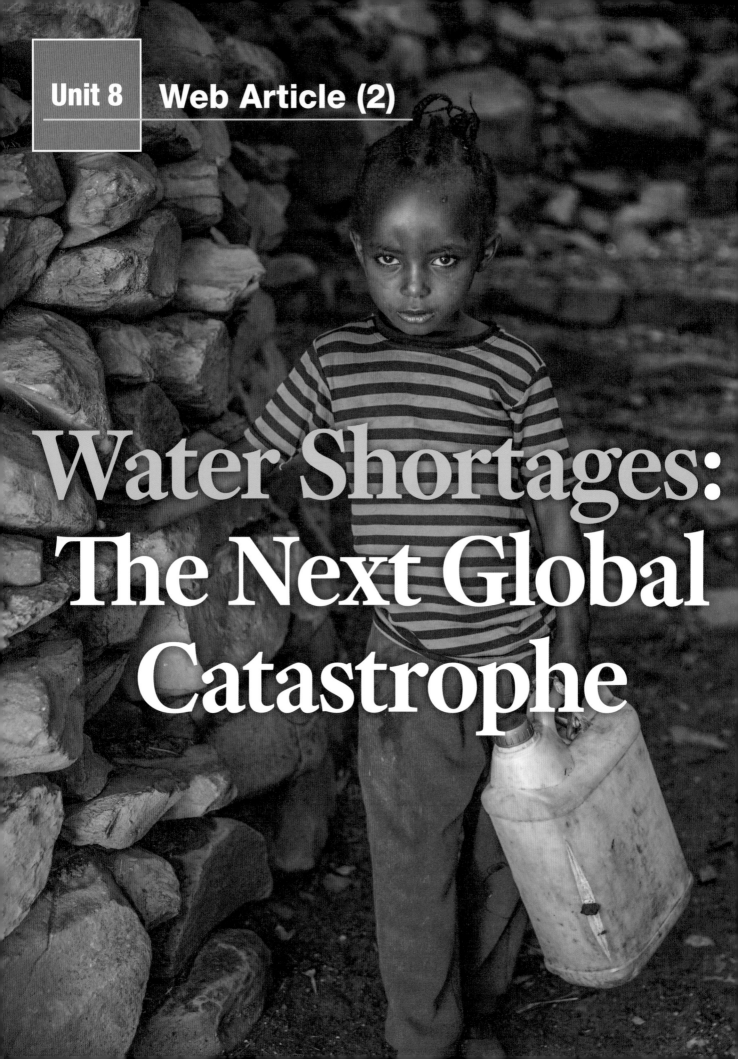

# Water Shortages: The Next Global Catastrophe

## Let's Get Started

### A. Before You Read

1. We use water for a lot more than just drinking. Write a check mark in the boxes for the ways in which you utilize water on a daily basis.

2. In a group or with a partner, list the ways you think people waste the most water. What can people do to save more water?

### B. Words in Context

🎵 CD 2-10

Use the words from the box to complete the following sentences. Change the word form if necessary.

| | | | |
|---|---|---|---|
| famine | imminent | call upon | livestock |
| insufficient | terrorism | necessity | produce |

1. If we don't do something to protect these critically endangered species, they will face the risk of _____ extinction.

2. During the _____, thousands of people tragically died because of a lack of food.

3. Food, water, and shelter—each of these is a(n) _____ for life.

4. Some farmers only grow crops, but others raise _____.

5. I like to go to the local farmers' market to shop for fresh _____ straight from the farm.

6. Due to global _____, security at airports, especially in the US, is tighter than ever.

7. Government officials have _____ the public to provide any information they might have about the criminals.

8. The company had to turn down the large order because of _____ resources.

2-11~18

Water scarcity is a crisis that the world's most powerful governments and figures are aware of, and yet it rarely seems to be spoken of by world leaders. Like other global issues, such as war, famine, and terrorism, it has the terrible power to wipe humans and other living creatures off the face of the earth. Now, as more and
5 more experts are calling upon the public and government officials to solve this problem, more countries have started to take action.

According to Seth Siegel, activist and author of the book *Let There Be Water: Israel's Solution for a Water-Starved World*, it is highly likely that by the year 2025, water could be a scarce resource on 60 percent of the world's landmasses. This
10 imminent crisis could cause billions of people around the world to face water-stressed conditions.

As an expert on the subject of water scarcity, Siegel has been invited to lecture at conferences around the world. In India alone, he points out, there are 600 million people who are using water systems that are projected to fail within a
15 decade. In Mexico and South America, a further 15 million people are in danger of having their water supply dry up altogether. Some people may think the water shortage is a Third World problem, but it actually impacts the world on a much more massive scale.

In a time when the world's economies are irrevocably intertwined, so too are
20 its food supply networks, which are vulnerable to the water shortage as well. A good portion of the food appearing on supermarket shelves in First World countries is grown and harvested in the Third World, where low labor costs keep prices down. A global water shortage, says Siegel, would in turn lead to a vast increase in the price of food everywhere.

What, one might ask, could be the cause of this cross-national water

Water scarcity

25

30

With less water, we produce less food.

shortage? The answer, according to Siegel, is climate change. With a rise in the
average global temperature, which scientists have concluded is impacted by the
industrial activities of humans, the main focus has been on issues such as rising sea
levels due to melting ice caps. What has been lost in the discussion, however, is the
way in which rain patterns have been altered. In certain areas, among them vitally
important food producing regions, the average rainfall has dwindled dramatically,
greatly reducing the ability to grow crops and raise livestock. Thus, a water shortage
also becomes a food shortage. 35

One country that could potentially help the world weather the storm of a
water crisis is Japan. The mountainous
country, which loses much of its fresh water
supply to the sea, is used to dealing with a
shortage of this necessity of life. Globally, an
average maximum of 8,000 cubic meters of
fresh water is available to every person per
year. In Japan, that figure is closer to 3,000
cubic meters. In parts of Tokyo, the amount of 40

 45

**Notes**

**vitally** *adv.* in a way that is exremely important
**dwindle** *v.* to decrease; to become smaller or weaker

Drip irrigation helps save more water than traditional irrigation systems.

water available per person is almost equivalent to that in northern Africa or the Middle East. To cope with this difficult situation, Japanese companies and factories
50 have come up with many innovative devices. One popular product is the Bubble90, a water-saving nozzle which can reduce the amount of water used in washing by as much as 95 percent. The nozzle can be attached to almost any kind of faucet, and it is now being used in restaurants, schools, and factories around Japan.

Another country that leads the way with its water-saving technology is
55 Israel. With 60 percent of its land composed of desert, this thirsty nation has strived to solve its water crisis for years. Israel has built desalination plants to turn sea water into fresh drinking water, and it recycles 85 percent of its sewage and uses it for agriculture. Perhaps its most remarkable innovation is its drip irrigation, also known as micro-irrigation. Instead of using a large amount of water to flood
60 fields, drip irrigation uses pipes to deliver water and drop it directly on every plant's roots. This way of growing crops uses 75 percent less water than traditional irrigation systems, and it can also yield more produce.

Today, Israel no longer has to worry about having an insufficient water supply, and it also serves as a great example for other countries that are trying to
65 reduce their water consumption. For most of us, however, perhaps the most efficient way to tackle this global crisis is to reduce the amount of water we use in our everyday lives.

## Notes

**faucet**  n.  a device for turning on or off a stream of liquid
**desalination**  n.  the process of removing salt from sea water so that it can be used for drinking or watering crops
**sewage**  n.  wastewater from homes, factories, or other buildings

# Reading Comprehension

**Multiple Choice:** Based on the reading, choose the best answer to each question.

**DETAIL** 1. According to Seth Siegel, what could happen by 2025?
    a. Billions of people will starve to death.
    b. 600 million people will live in the Third World.
    c. Water will have disappeared almost entirely from the planet.
    d. Water could be hard to find in the majority of the world.

**PURPOSE** 2. Why does the author say that water shortages are not just a Third World problem?
    a. Because there is no such thing as the Third World
    b. Because water shortages have already occurred all over the world
    c. Because water shortages can also cause food shortages in the First World
    d. Because people in the Third World may move to First World countries

**IDIOM** 3. What does "weather the storm" in Line 39 most likely mean?
    a. To be safe from harm or damage
    b. To get away from something without receiving any punishment
    c. To create more rainfall
    d. To avoid bad weather

**INFERENCE** 4. What can be said about the amount of water available to people in Japan each year?
    a. It is steadily rising.
    b. It is quite low.
    c. It is above average.
    d. It is in line with the global average.

**DETAIL** 5. Which of the following is NOT used in Israel to save water?
    a. Recycled sewage
    b. Desalination plants
    c. Water-saving nozzles
    d. Drip irrigation

**DETAIL** 6. Which country is learning to reduce water consumption from Israel?
    a. Japan
    b. Mexico
    c. India
    d. We don't know.

**Think More**

1. Have you been impacted by a water shortage? If so, describe what happened. If not, describe what could happen.

2. Do you think each of us has a responsibility to conserve water? Why or why not?

# Reading Skill  Understanding Cause and Effect

Sometimes an article may contain a cause-and-effect relationship, which usually gives reasons and explanations for certain siuations or events. This relationship can be revealed by key words, such as *because*, *due to*, *therefore*, *thus*, *so*, *consequently*, *as a result*, etc. Understanding cause and effect will help readers to see how the main points and details are put together in a paragraph or article.

**Task 1:** Read the short passage and fill in the cause and effect in the chart below.

The declining rainfall each year has caused many places around the world to suffer from water shortages. Taiwan, unfortunately, is one of them. In 2017, Taiwan recorded its lowest rainfall in 70 years between August and September and its second lowest rainfall in 54 years in winter. As a result, Taiwan's Water Resources Agency began implementing first-phase water rationing in several cities in southern Taiwan. At the same time, goverment officials also tried to raise public awareness about the importance of saving water. However, the public didn't seem to show much concern over this issue since water only costs about one fifth the global average.

| Cause | → | Effect |
|---|---|---|
| | → | Many places around the world are suffering from water shortages. |
| The rainfall recorded in Taiwan in 2017 was severely low (in the fall and the winter). | → | 1.<br><br>2. |

**Task 2:** Read the fifth paragraph of Reading and answer the following questions.

1. What is causing a rise in the average global temperature?

_____

2. What situation may melting ice caps lead to?

_____

3. How does a water shortage become a food shortage?

_____

# Vocabulary Builder  The Suffix *-age*

The suffix *-age* can be combined with nouns, adjectives, and verbs. It indicates the status of something, an action or the outcome of something, a collection of something, a fee, or a place. In Reading, we saw the word *shortage*. Other examples include *wastage*, *baggage*, *postage*, and *orphanage*.

**Task 1:** Match the words to the correct definitions.

1. coverage •

2. breakage •

3. dosage •

4. marriage •

5. patronage •

• something that becomes broken

• financial support given to someone or an organization

• the amount of medicine that should be taken each time

• the state of two people joining their lives in a legal union

• the activity of reporting an event on TV or in newspapers

**Task 2:** Complete the sentences with the words from the box. Not all of them will be used.

| lineage | passage | storage | blockage | acreage | brokerage | mileage |

1. One-third of this national park's _____ is woodlands.

2. After their baby was born, the young couple moved to a larger house, since their old house didn't have enough space or _____.

3. There was a(n) _____ in a water pipe in Wendy's house, so she asked a plumber to come and fix it.

4. Stacy's new boyfriend can trace his _____ back to a wealthy noble family in England.

## Let's Think About It!

In this unit we looked an important issue the world is facing today. Now we're going to brainstorm some solutions to various global issues. First, form a group of four to six students and discuss the main factors involved in the issues listed. Finally, with your teammates, try to draft some possible solutions, and then share your ideas with other groups. You may frame these solutions either from the point of view of individuals or the government. You can also add a different issue that you think it is important to discuss.

| Global Issue | What/Who Caused the Problem? | Possible Solution |
|---|---|---|
| Water shortages | • Climate change<br>• People using too much water | • Decrease individual water consumption<br>• Decrease greenhouse gas emissions to counter effects of climate change |
| Plastic waste in oceans | | |
| High unemployment rates | | |
| | | |

# The Hippie Movement

## Let's Get Started

### A. Before You Read

1. Look at the following pictures and match them to the names of the subcultures below.

2. Which of the subcultures above interests you the most? Why?

### B. Words in Context

 2-19

Use the words from the box to complete the following sentences. Change the word form if necessary.

| | | | |
|---|---|---|---|
| chant | barefoot | alienated | rimless |
| synonymous | hold on to | erupt | rally |

1. A large _____ was held to call for changes to the gun-ownership laws.

2. For many people, Hakodate Morning Market is _____ with tasty seafood.

3. When we got to the beach, we took off our shoes and ran _____ on the sand.

4. Many people feel that a large-scale war may soon _____ in the troubled Middle East.

5. If you want to show support for our cause, please _____ along with us during the protest.

6. Sometimes, social media causes people to feel _____ from their peers.

7. Sue wanted to dress up as a hippie for the costume party, so she bought _____ glasses and a long dress.

8. Tom always acts independently and _____ the belief that being different is what makes a person special.

*Peace and love*

2-20~25

In the classic American movie *Forrest Gump*, Forrest and his childhood friend Jenny had an emotional reunion in the Reflecting Pool of the Lincoln Memorial in Washington, D.C. Before they met again, Jenny had left her hometown and become involved in the hippie movement. During that time, many young people were sent 5 to Vietnam to fight in war. That was why Jenny, a hippie at that time, took part in an antiwar rally in Washington, D.C., and was able to meet up with Forrest again there.

A "hippie" refers to a member of a countercultural movement that sprang up during the 1960s and 1970s. The movement originally emerged out of the earlier 10 beatnik movement in the 1950s. The word "hippie" came from "hipster," a term that was used to describe a youth who tried to reject mainstream life and stood against social conformity. The roots of the hippie movement can be traced back to the Haight-Ashbury district of San Francisco, California. Back then, there was a group of young people who didn't feel they fitted in with society, which mainly held on to 15 conservative values. These young people also rejected the paradigm of unquestioning compliance and wanted to question everything that society held dear.

One way for the hippies to show their dissatisfaction with society was by dressing differently than others. The hippies wore casual long dresses, bell-20 bottomed blue jeans, and baggy tie-dyed T-shirts in "psychedelic" colors. They

---

**Notes**

**countercultural** *adj.* going against the culture of mainstream society
**beatnik** *n.* a young person in the 1950s who rejected the traditions of society
**paradigm** *n.* a pattern or model
**bell-bottomed** *adj.* describing pants that are very wide at the ankle
**baggy** *adj.* describing clothing that is very loose-fitting
**psychedelic** *adj.* having bright colors and unusual patterns; relating to drugs that produce hallucinations

A group of hippies

enjoyed wearing sandals or even going barefoot. Men grew their hair and beards long, and women, also long-haired, wore beaded necklaces and rimless granny glasses. They expressed themselves this way because they often felt alienated from middle-class society, which the hippies thought of as being dominated by materialism and repression. For the hippies, it was essential to be distinctive and free, not only in their outer appearance, but also in their inner spirit. 25

30

To expand on the idea of opening their minds in a world which, according to the hippies' perception, was becoming increasingly closed-minded, they often sought spiritual guidance from Eastern philosophy and religions, particularly Buddhism. They also sought aid from psychedelic and hallucinogenic drugs, such as marijuana and LSD. For the hippies, the practice of taking "head trips" helped them free their mind and expand their consciousness. At the same time, since the hippies advocated a peaceful and natural lifestyle, they protested against the Vietnam War, which had erupted in 1955 and continued for the next 20 years. To show their support for world peace, the hippies often displayed the peace symbol on many things. In addition, one of the popular phrases of that time was "Make love, not war." Basically, the hippies did many things that were considered unacceptable by mainstream society, such as parading through the streets chanting antiwar slogans and phrases promoting the virtues of peace and love. 35

40

45

When they protested the war, the hippies usually held public gatherings that featured bands and groups of musicians expressing their encouragement of freedom. Folk and psychedelic rock 'n' roll music were both important parts of the hippie culture, and singers like Bob Dylan and bands such as the Beatles, the Grateful Dead, and the 50

## Notes

**beaded** *adj.* decorated with small pieces of glass, wood, etc. that have holes through them so that they can be put on a string and worn as jewelry

**materialism** *n.* a belief that money and physical possessions are the most valuable things in life

**hallucinogenic** *adj.* describing a type of drug that makes a person see things that are not there

The peace symbol

Rolling Stones were closely connected with the hippie movement. In 1967, over
55 100,000 people traveled to San Francisco and gathered in the Haight-Ashbury
district to protest against the war, enjoy the music, or simply celebrate life, and this
became known as the Summer of Love. Most of the hippies wore flowers in their
hair to express their love of nature, so they were called "flower children." This also
led to the famous phrase "flower power." Later in 1969, a three-day music festival
60 was held in rural New York and attracted more than 400,000 people. It was known
as the Woodstock Music and Art Fair, or simply Woodstock. Woodstock was
regarded by many people as a pivotal moment in popular music history, and this
major event became virtually synonymous with the hippie movement.

As the 1970s came around, the hippie culture faced doubt and
65 disillusionment. The glow of peace and love faded as the Vietnam War raged on and
American soldiers continued to die for a cause few believed in. It became
increasingly apparent that the ideal world that the hippies had envisioned—one in
which everyone lived together in peace and harmony—was little more than a pipe
dream. However, it's important to note that the hippie movement occurred not
70 only in the US but also in many other countries, such as Canada, the UK, Australia,
Mexico, and even in Japan. It also had an influence on popular music, literature,
art, fashion, and so on. The concept of going back to nature also helped in the
growth of interest in health foods and environmental protection. It's safe to say
that the spirit of the hippies lives on, and the hippie culture will likely remain one
75 of history's important subcultures.

## Notes

**pivotal** *adj.* very important or influential
**disillusionment** *n.* a feeling of disappointment
**envision** *v.* to think that something will happen or come true

# Reading Comprehension

**Multiple Choice:** Based on the reading, choose the best answer to each question.

PURPOSE 1. What is the main purpose of this article?

   a. To criticize a certain lifestyle and its principles

   b. To provide an overview of a broad social movement

   c. To describe the atmosphere of a particular place and time

   d. To discuss the flaws and merits of a particular way of life

DETAIL 2. Which of the following is NOT true about the hippies?

   a. They liked to wear clothes in a variety of bright colors.

   b. They preferred to keep their hair long and listen to rock 'n' roll music.

   c. They forbade the use of all kinds of drugs at their gatherings.

   d. They promoted the idea of love and peace.

INFERENCE 3. What year did the Vietnam War end?

   a. 1955

   b. 1967

   c. 1970

   d. 1975

DETAIL 4. Why did people call the hippies "flower children"?

   a. They used flowers to show their support for world peace.

   b. They sent flowers to people in other countries.

   c. They traveled with their children.

   d. They grew flowers and sold them to others.

PHRASE 5. What does "a pipe dream" in Lines 68–69 mean?

   a. a possible solution

   b. a horrible nightmare

   c. a positive result

   d. a vain hope

TONE 6. What is the overall tone of this article?

   a. Skeptical

   b. Combative

   c. Informative

   d. Sympathetic

**Think More**

1. Do you agree with the hippie lifestyle or hippie culture? Why or why not?

2. What kind of lifestyle do you wish to have? What do you think you have to do to achieve it?

## Reading Skill  Recognizing the Chronological Sequence

When the information in a passage or text is organized in the order of time, it is written in chronological order. The root word *chrono* means "time," while *logic* refers to "order." The author sometimes gives the exact time or date, but sometimes the author does not say the time exactly. In order to recognize the chronological sequence, you should focus on finding exact dates, years, or keywords, such as *after*, *before*, *during*, *finally*, *meanwhile*, etc., so that you have an idea of what the basic timeline is.

**Task 1:** Read the following passage and number the sequence of the events by filling in 1, 2, 3, and 4.

Charlotte is really busy in October. She has to finish a large-scale project by the 6th and then give a presentation on the 11th. After that, she needs to visit some important clients in the middle of the month. Then, before she goes on a business trip to Italy at the end of the month, she still has to take care of some work and attend three meetings.

(     ) Visit some important clients        (     ) Give a presentation

(     ) Go on a business trip to Italy       (     ) Finish a large-scale project

**Task 2:** Read through the second and fourth paragraph of Reading and then fill in the time of the following events.

1. The hippie movement: _____

2. The beatnik movement: _____

3. Vietnam War: _____

## Vocabulary Builder  The Prefix *anti-*

The prefix *anti-* means "opposed to, opposite of, or against," and it is used to form nouns or adjectives. In Reading, we saw the example *antiwar*, meaning "opposed to a war." One thing to note is that the prefix *anti-* is often hyphenated in some of the words that it forms. For example, *antiwar* and anti-war can both be found in dictionaries.

**Task 1:** Which of the following words can take the prefix *anti-*? Write the prefix in the space for those which can take it or put an "X" in front of the words which can't.

1. ____productive     2. ____democracy     3. ____climax     4. ____act

5. ____hero       6. ____tank        7. ____part       8. ____matter

**Task 2:** Use the words from the box to complete the sentences. Change the word form if necessary.

| antibiotic | antipersonnel | antisocial |
| --- | --- | --- |

1. Until all of the _____ mines in this area are removed, no one will be allowed to enter.

2. After an in-depth investigation, the police were able to determine that the suspect had an _____ personality.

3. The vet treated the sick dog with _____ and anti-inflammatory drugs.

# Let's Think About It!

We have learned about the hippie movement, and we have also learned that many hippies used the peace symbol to show their support of love and peace. The following chart explains what the symbol represents and how it was designed.

Now, divide into groups of four students. After taking a look at the meaning of the peace symbol, create a new symbol for a topic that your group chooses by answering the questions below. Your topic can be a subculture like punk, or it can be a concept like "going green."

|  |  | (Draw your own symbol here.) |
|---|---|---|
| **What does the symbol mean?** | • Nuclear disarmament<br>• Antiwar<br>• Peace | |
| **How is it designed?** | It combines two letter of the semaphore signals "N" and "D," which stand for "nuclear disarmament." | |
| **When can we use it?** | • (Nuclear) disarmament movement<br>• Antiwar movement<br>• Showing support of peace and love | |

# Time to Put the Brakes on Fast Fashion

## Let's Get Started

### A. Before You Read

1. Do you often shop for clothes? Where do you usually buy them?

2. What are the advantages and disadvantages of online shopping compared to shopping at a regular store? Use the table below to list some of the pros and cons.

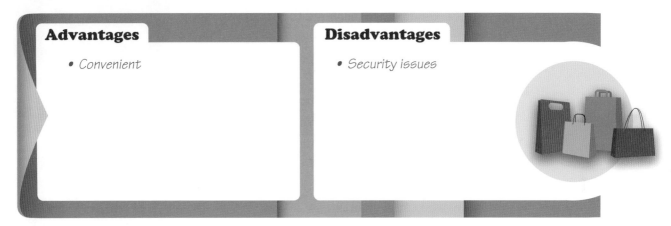

**Advantages**

• Convenient

**Disadvantages**

• Security issues

3. Have you heard of the phrase "fast fashion"? If so, what do you know about it? If not, what do you think it might mean?

### B. Words in Context

 2-26

Use the words from the box to complete the following sentences. Change the word form if necessary.

| modification | inspection | boom | pact |
|---|---|---|---|
| ethical | linger | optimistic | wardrobe |

1. After yesterday's meeting, several colleagues _____ in the room to go over some of the issues.

2. With these _____, the company has made this device more popular than the previous model.

3. These days, many corporations must consider the _____ concerns of consumers.

4. The two countries signed a(n) _____ to increase trade and economic activity.

5. The movie theater was closed after it failed a safety _____ yesterday.

6. Although many people worry about the future, I am _____ about what will happen in the years to come.

7. The company is trying to understand the _____ in popularity of online games among young people.

8. I went shopping last night because I wanted to add some new clothes to my _____.

2-27~34

The advent of fast fashion over the last couple of decades has brought stylish garments to the masses at affordable prices. Brands such as ZARA, H&M, and Uniqlo have mastered the art of getting

5  the latest trends from the catwalk to the consumer at breakneck speed. Whereas new product lines were seasonal previously, the cycle has now been reduced to just a few weeks. This is great for shoppers, as they get to update their wardrobes on a regular basis

10  instead of having to wear the same old clothes. Meanwhile, clothing manufacturers are selling more products than ever before. With such a win-win situation, who could object?

If only life were that simple. The reality is

15  there's an ugly side to the fast fashion industry. In fact, there are several ugly sides. To begin with, there are the clothes themselves. Statistics provided by Greenpeace indicate that 1.7 million metric tons of chemicals are used annually in the dyeing process.

20  The environmental organization further warns that a significant percentage of these are hazardous chemicals. Environmentalists are particularly worried about a group of chemicals known as PFCs. These are extremely resistant to biological breakdown, meaning they can linger in our atmosphere for centuries. The production of outdoor clothing

25  relies heavily on PFCs as they can be used for waterproofing and other protective purposes.

Natural materials are also a major cause for concern, with the cotton industry coming in for sustained criticism. Around 11–12 percent of the world's pesticides are used to cultivate cotton crops, and these cause serious damage to

30  water sources, particularly in the developing world. Furthermore, the water used to produce cotton-based items is a huge drain on the Earth's resources. To take just

## Notes

**advent**  *n.*  the beginning or introduction of something important
**catwalk**  *n.*  the long platform at a fashion show
**breakneck**  *adj.*  very fast or dangerous
**waterproofing**  *n.*  the act or process of making something not be damaged by water

Rana Plaza collapse, 2013

one example: The process of making one cotton T-shirt requires 2,700 liters of water. That's three times the amount consumed by the average person in a year! The boom in demand that has accompanied fast fashion has only increased these threats to the environment. A further issue concerns waste. Although 80 billion    35
items of clothing are produced each year, three quarters of these are burned or put in landfills—locations where garbage is buried. Only 25 percent are recycled.

More immediate than the environmental impact, though, are the dangers faced by millions of workers employed in the clothing industry. Here, again, fast fashion has been accused of making an already serious problem even worse. As    40
companies strive to outdo their competitors by continually slashing turnover times, the pressure to meet deadlines can have disastrous consequences. The most shocking example came in April 2013 when a large garment factory in Bangladesh collapsed, killing over 1,000 people. Companies based at the Rana Plaza, as the building was known, produced clothing for many international brands, including    45
Benetton and Wal-Mart. Although cracks had started to appear in the walls of the building the day before, workers were told that there was no risk. Managers of one of the companies even threatened to withhold the employees' salaries if they didn't show up for work.

In response, several companies have said they are powerless to influence    50
construction and safety standards in countries to which they outsource their

## Notes

**outdo** *v.* to perform better than others
**slash** *v.* to greatly reduce
**withhold** *v.* to refuse to release or give something
**outsource** *v.* to ask another company or another country to provide goods and services

operations, but they would focus on improving working conditions for employees. Do these claims stand up? Let's look at the evidence. Following the Rana Plaza disaster, a legally binding agreement was established to enforce better monitoring
55 of safety standards. The initiative calls for independent safety inspections. It also requires companies to contribute toward the cost of upgrading facilities to ensure their workers are safe. Spanish brand ZARA, Swedish brand H&M, and other European brands like Benetton signed up, as did several US companies, including Calvin Klein and Tommy Hilfiger. However, most American firms ignored the pact.

60 Noticeable by their absence were Wal-Mart and Gap among other multinationals. The former company, which is the world's largest retailer, said the agreement was impractical. "We are talking about 4,500 factories," Wal-Mart said in a statement taken from a meeting on the issue. "In most cases very extensive and costly modifications would need to be undertaken. It is not financially feasible for
65 the brands to make such investments." Critics could be forgiven for not buying this argument because the company's net income for the previous year had been US$17 billion.

With profits and customer satisfaction now sky-high, it seems that the fast fashion train is unstoppable. However, it also appears that no one is at the wheel of
70 this enormous, powerful vehicle. Is there any way of slowing it down before permanent damage is caused? There are reasons to be optimistic. Many consumers are starting to buy their clothes from companies who promote more ethical manufacturing practices. Some are realizing that they might not need to own quite so many garments. There has also been an increase in repairing, recycling, and even
75 upcycling clothes.

In the end, though, the fast fashion phenomenon is driven as much by the manufacturers as the consumers. After all, it was they that first came up with the idea of speeding things up. If consumer shopping trends are to change, they are likely to do so when the big brands decide to apply the brakes.

**Notes**

**feasible** *adj.* describing something that can be done or achieved
**upcycle** *v.* to reuse something to create something new

# Reading Comprehension

**Multiple Choice:** Based on the reading, choose the best answer to each question.

**VOCABULARY**
1. In Lines 12–13, "a win-win situation" means a situation _____.
   a. where everyone makes money
   b. where everyone gets a prize
   c. where everyone benefits
   d. where everyone competes

**DETAIL**
2. What is NOT mentioned as an environmental problem caused by the clothing industry?
   a. Water pollution
   b. Dangerous chemicals
   c. Overuse of natural resources
   d. Damage to crops

**DETAIL**
3. What is true of PFCs?
   a. They take a long time to disappear.
   b. They help protect clothing manufacturers.
   c. They contain high levels of water.
   d. They are found only outdoors.

**DETAIL**
4. Based on the fourth paragraph, why is there pressure to meet deadlines?
   a. Because those workers face dangers
   b. Because suppliers don't ensure safety
   c. Because other companies are working faster
   d. Because employees need to earn more money

**INFERENCE**
5. What does the author think about Wal-Mart's claims?
   a. They are fair.
   b. They are not true.
   c. They are accurate.
   d. They are hard to assess.

**TONE**
6. What best describes the author's depiction of fast fashion in the last paragraph?
   a. Dangerous and out of control
   b. Thrilling and enjoyable
   c. Expensive and complicated
   d. Mechanical and slow

**Think More**

1. Will fast fashion remain popular in the future? What could change the trend?

2. Do manufacturers have a duty to maintain ethical standards? How can they be made to stick to these principles?

## Reading Skill | Interpreting Tone and Rhetorical Questions

Some authors might introduce a subject from one point of view only to criticize or argue against that view later in the article. Words of contrast, such as *yet*, *while*, and *though*, are obvious signals of this. Elsewhere, the clues might be more subtle. The author might imply something through tone or else pose a rhetorical question. This is a question which might not need an answer and is used for effect.

**Task 1:** Read the following passage. Circle the author's tone (for/against) and give reason(s) for your answer.

Nowadays, many people get their news from the Internet. This is understandable, as links to news reports are easy to post and share with friends. There is also a greater variety of sources than ever before. To many, there seem to be no downsides to this.

I think the author is for/against news from the Internet.

Reason(s): _____

_____

_____

**Task 2:** Look at the first paragraph of Reading and answer the following question.

Which of the following positions is the author most likely to take in the article?
a. Fast fashion will become increasingly popular.
b. There are some negative aspects of fast fashion.
c. Fast fashion is the best solution for customers.
d. The pros of fast fashion outweigh the cons.

## Vocabulary Builder | The Suffix *-ish*

The suffix *-ish* can be used with adjectives to imply that a noun possesses certain characteristics. Thus, the adjective *stylish*, which appeared in Reading, suggests the garments have style. The suffix *-ish* can also be used to form adjectives that express a particular place. For example, we also saw the words *Spanish* and *Swedish*, which respectively mean "coming from Spain" and "coming from Sweden."

**Task:** Complete the following sentences by choosing the correct words.

1. It was very _____ of Luke to hide his sister's laptop under the sofa. It was really immature!
   a. stylish          b. Spanish          c. childish          d. reddish

2. Many people think Istanbul is the _____ capital, but the capital is, in fact, Ankara.
   a. Swedish          b. British          c. Scottish          d. Turkish

3. Because Sue is so _____ and spoiled, it's no wonder that she doesn't have any friends.
   a. youngish          b. selfish          c. stylish          d. Swedish

4. It was really _____ of me to lock my keys in my car.
   a. British          b. childish          c. stylish          d. foolish

## Let's Think About It!

In Reading, upcycling is mentioned as a way of dealing with the issue of fast fashion. What could unwanted items of clothing be used to create? Work in groups and come up with ideas for how to give old garments a new lease on life. If you can, think of as many ways as possible to use old clothes to make new things. Use the table below to list your ideas.

| Use | Benefits | Potential Difficulties |
|---|---|---|
| Household decorations such as curtains, bedsheets, covers, etc. | Can create interesting, colorful designs using a variety of material | Requires sewing skills |
| | | |
| | | |
| | | |

# From Pictures to Words: The Evolution of Jimmy Liao

## A. Before You Read

1. What kinds of images do you expect to find in the following types of reading materials? Complete the table with some of your own ideas.

| Children's Literature | Travel Magazines | Science Textbooks |
|---|---|---|
| • animals | • scenery | • diagrams |

2. Do you know any picture books that are famous for their illustrations? Introduce to your partner a picture book that you enjoy reading.

## B. Words in Context

 2-35

Use the words from the box to complete the following sentences. Change the word form if necessary.

| | | | |
|---|---|---|---|
| sensitivity | inclination | plea | unfold |
| moving | render | manuscript | narrative |

1. You have to be patient with this novel as the plot _____ rather slowly.

2. Responding to _____ by many of her fans, the singer decided to come out of retirement.

3. Some philosophical works are hard to _____ into simple language.

4. I have no _____ to work on my thesis today, so I think I'll just take a break.

5. All _____ for the creative writing competition should be submitted by the end of the month.

6. The speaker showed great _____ to the audience with his thoughtful and kind words.

7. The story has a fast-moving _____ that really holds the reader's attention.

8. The teacher's _____ story about her poor childhood made all the students in the class burst into tears.

🔊 2-36~40

If, as the well-known saying goes, a picture is worth a thousand words, Jimmy Liao has created the equivalent of the complete works of Shakespeare. The award-winning Taiwanese illustrator has now published over 50 picture books full of his distinctive art. Liao has made his name by creating his own unique worlds featuring characters lost in magical but occasionally mournful landscapes. Yet, while he is best known for his images, Liao has also mastered the art of written storytelling. He has contributed text to most of his books, and his words have now been rendered into dozens of foreign tongues. This success is all the more deserving of praise when one considers the obstacles Liao has encountered.

Liao was not always so confident with the textual side of things. Having spent more than a decade at an advertising firm, followed by a spell working for newspapers, he was used to letting other people do the writing. Liao said that while he had great admiration for writers, he did not believe himself to be blessed with any talent for the written word. In fact, despite the pleas of friends, he lacked the confidence to even put a collection of his pictures into storybook form. It took a life-threatening illness to change Liao's perspective. In 1995, he was diagnosed with leukemia. While battling this form of cancer, he was asked by a book company to submit a manuscript for publication. It might seem like a paradox, but Liao credits his battle to overcome the disease with inspiring him. Determined to defeat the cancer, he was nevertheless still fearful that the worst might come to pass. If it should, he wanted to leave something behind for his wife and young daughter to remember him by.

### Notes

**mournful** *adj.* sad or melancholy
**textual** *adj.* relating to written words in a text
**leukemia** *n.* a type of cancer that affects the blood

His first inclination was to compose something from all of his existing work. Looking over his old drawings, however, he soon realized that these didn't quite fit the bill. Liao was carrying a heavy burden in his heart, and he felt he had so much more to unleash. Something else was required if he was to properly capture his emotions. He found what he was looking for in a small illustration that he had created to accompany the work of Hsiao Yeh, a famous Taiwanese novelist and screenwriter. Detecting the makings of a story in this little drawing of a girl skipping through the woods, he began to ask himself questions. "Who is she?" "Where is she going?" "Does she feel happy or sad?" In answering these questions, Liao was able to produce a series of pictures from which a story gradually unfolded. Seated at his desk, Liao would gaze out of his window and imagine what his little heroine might be doing out there.

With no structure in mind, Liao would move on to the next frame only when he had finished the previous picture. By the end of three months, he felt he had a complete work in place. The publisher disagreed and insisted that words be added to the images to create a more obvious story. Liao was stumped. His medium had

35

40

45

**Notes**

**unleash** *v.* to release (especially a powerful force)
**stumped** *adj.* unable to find an answer or solve a problem

Illustration from *The Sound of Colors*

50

55

always been visual, and he felt completely unqualified to work with words. "I rarely used words to express my ideas," he said. Searching for inspiration, he purchased collections of poetry and tried reading as much as possible. It was to no avail. Then, by chance, he bumped into an expert in children's literature and learning. Her techniques involve encouraging kids to look at pictures and read sentences out loud, describing what they see. Drawing on these methods, Liao began reciting his feelings aloud while looking at his pictures. Sentence followed sentence and eventually Liao had a poetic narrative to fit his illustrations. Released in 1998, the picture book was the best-selling *Secrets in the Woods*.

60

Shortly after the completion of his first publication, Liao received some wonderful news. His medical treatment had been successful, and he was free of the leukemia. His own personal story is even more moving than the tales that spring from his imagination. In coming through a period that could have ended his life, he was able to create a work of great sensitivity and beauty.

**Note**

**to no avail** *idiom* failing to achieve what is wanted

# Reading Comprehension

**Multiple Choice:** Based on the reading, choose the best answer to each question.

**DETAIL**

1. What is true of Jimmy Liao's books?
   a. They don't usually contain words.
   b. They contain text and images.
   c. They teach people magic.
   d. They feature photographs of scenery.

**FIGURATIVE LANGUAGE**

2. What does the author mean by saying Liao has created the equivalent of the complete works of Shakespeare?
   a. He writes in an old-fashioned way.
   b. He has produced dramatic works.
   c. He has done a lot of writing.
   d. He has drawn many pictures.

**INFERENCE**

3. Why might Liao's reaction to the cancer seem like a paradox?
   a. Because a negative situation led to a positive outcome
   b. Because he wasn't writing about illness in his books
   c. Because he felt happy in spite of his sickness
   d. Because he was confused about his situation

**DETAIL**

4. Why did Liao NOT use any of the old drawings he first gathered?
   a. Because the quality wasn't good enough
   b. Because they didn't express his feelings
   c. Because they had already been published
   d. Because an expert in children's literature wanted them

**PHRASE**

5. In Line 54, the phrase "drawing on" is closest in meaning to _____.
   a. changing
   b. ignoring
   c. utilizing
   d. developing

**TONE**

6. How does the author feel about Jimmy Liao's story?
   a. Touched
   b. Shocked
   c. Distressed
   d. Skeptical

**Think More**

1. Have you ever read any of Jimmy Liao's picture books? If so, what did you think about them?

2. Can you think of any other famous people who have overcome obstacles to achieve something? How did they do it?

# Reading Skill    Interpreting an Author's Values

When reading a text, it can be useful to consider what kind of beliefs and values an author might be expressing. Sometimes the author might just present facts. Other times, he or she might give an opinion that expresses his or her personal values. Learning to distinguish between the two can be helpful.

**Task 1:** Look at following sentences and choose the best word to describe the author's values. The first one has been done for you.

1. These humanitarian efforts fool nobody. Everyone knows exactly what kind of company this is.
   → _d_

2. You may not like Peter, but you can't deny his qualities as an athlete. → _____

3. What could be Ivy's reason for making such claims? One has to wonder. → _____

4. To have overcome the odds and turned things around like that is nothing short of a miracle.
   → _____

**Task 2:** Look at the first paragraph of Reading and answer the question.

What best describes the author's view of Liao's achievements?
a. Impatience          b. Confusion          c. Admiration          d. Determination

# Vocabulary Builder    The Suffix -*ique*

The suffix -*ique* comes from French, and it means "to have the nature of or be similar to something." It is an older version of the more common suffix -*ic*, and it is used with several nouns and adjectives in English. In Reading, we saw *unique*, which means "special" and *technique*, which refers to "a skill or a method of doing something."

**Task 1:** Match the words to the correct definitions.

1. antique •                          • a small store selling fashionable clothes
2. physique •                        • an old, often valuable item
3. critique •                          • a person's body shape
4. boutique •                        • a detailed analysis of an idea or work

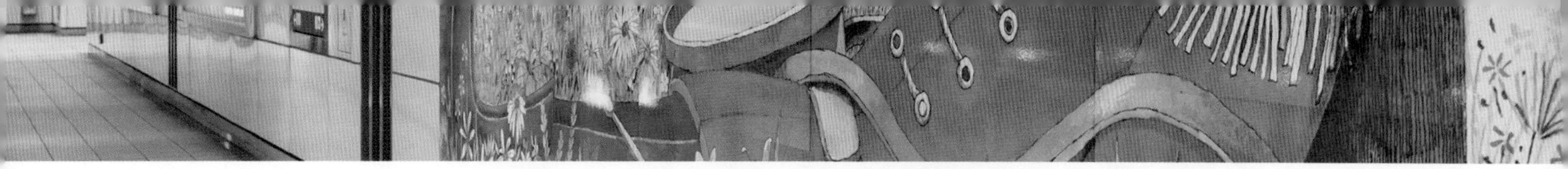

**Task 2:** Complete the sentences with the words with the suffix *-ique* from Reading or Task 1. Change the word form if necessary.

1. In his _____ of the theory, the philosopher raised several important arguments.

2. There are many trendy _____ in the lanes in this part of town.

3. The judges agreed that the violinist's _____ was almost perfect.

4. No one sounds quite like this singer, so she is considered to have a(n) _____ voice.

## Let's Think About It!

Could you tell a story without using words? Let's find out! First, with a partner, think of a story and then think about how you can present it in images. Then, in the box below, draw a series of four pictures that tells your story. When you have finished, present your drawings to another team and see if they can tell your story in their own words. Write down the other team's interpretations below each picture and then compare their plot with your own original story.

**Picture 1**

_____
_____

**Picture 2**

_____
_____

**Picture 3**

_____
_____

**Picture 4**

_____
_____

# Confronting Your Fears: How ERP Can Help Solve OCD

OBSESSIVE-COMPULSIVE DISORDER

# Let's Get Started

## A. Before You Read

1. Have you ever had a thought that you couldn't get out of your head? How did it make you feel?

2. Obsessive-compulsive disorder (OCD) is a condition that affects many people these days. Try to answer the following questions to see if you have any symptoms of OCD. Then, check your results below.

| | |
|---|---|
| 1. Are you frequently worried about germs and the possibility of catching a disease? | Yes / No |
| 2. Do you often worry about a loved one being harmed because of your actions? | Yes / No |
| 3. Do you ever feel the need to repeat actions over and over again? | Yes / No |
| 4. Do you collect useless items and have problems with throwing them away? | Yes / No |
| 5. Do you like keeping things perfectly arranged? | Yes / No |
| 6. Have you ever worried about doing bad things, such as harming a stranger? | Yes / No |
| 7. Do you tend to avoid certain numbers or words that are considered unlucky? | Yes / No |
| 8. Do you ever ask the same question several times even though you know the answer? | Yes / No |

**Your Score**

0–2 yes answers: You may have the occasional OCD thought, but no more than the average person.

3–5 yes answers: You are exhibiting some of the key signs of OCD behavior.

6–8 yes answers: There is a good chance you have an OCD personality.

## B. Words in Context

CD 2-41

Use the words from the box to complete the following sentences. Change the word form if necessary.

| | | | |
|---|---|---|---|
| submerge | passing | irrational | interval |
| trigger | compel | core | abbreviation |

1. Taking medication for an illness does not always address the _____ issue.

2. There was a 15-minute _____ between the two parts of the play.

3. I strongly suggest that you wear a helmet while riding your bike, but I can't _____ you to wear one.

4. After the accident, the ship remained half _____ in the water.

5. Many people think the two brothers look alike, but I feel there is only a(n) _____ resemblance.

6. The drop in share prices was _____ by the company's revised sales forecast.

7. Like OCD, a phobia is an anxiety disorder, which is characterized by a(n) _____ fear of something.

8. Some _____ are so common that people don't even know what the letters stand for.

2-42~48

*By Dr. Mohan Pradhan, M.D.*

If you're reading this first sentence, there's a good chance that you have at least a passing interest in psychology. If I'm right about that first assumption, you will probably be familiar with the abbreviation OCD. Afflicting an estimated 2.3
5　percent of adults between the ages of 18 and 54 in the United States, obsessive-compulsive disorder is among the most common mental health conditions. How about ERP? Those of you with a business background might be thinking of enterprise resource planning—a process for managing a business. Well, you'd be way off the mark. But, let's talk about OCD first.

10　A common misconception is that OCD refers specifically to actions, such as hand-washing, checking on doors and windows, and hoarding various items. While these could all be signs that someone is suffering from some form of OCD, they are actually just the symptoms, rather than the core of the problem itself. In fact, as the name suggests, OCD can be split into two distinct parts: obsession and
15　compulsion. The former afflicts all OCD sufferers and is at the root of the disorder, whereas the latter is not always present. All OCD stems from some kind of fear. These anxieties could be related to external threats or to potential harm to others caused by a sufferer's actions or even inaction. A person might be constantly plagued by irrational fears concerning germs. This is the obsessive component of
20　the disorder. In many cases, obsessions related to germs and cleanliness cause sufferers to wash their hands repeatedly over the course of a day, sometimes with the shortest of intervals. Acting out one's obsessions is the compulsive aspect of OCD.

25　Now, some of you might ask, isn't what we're describing here just a regular phobia? There are indeed a lot of similarities between phobias and OCD. For a start, both

## Notes

**afflict** *v.* to cause pain or suffering
**obsessive-compulsive** *adj.* relating to a condition where people are abnormally focused on one particular thing and/or cannot stop a certain behavior
**misconception** *n.* an incorrect opinion based on a misunderstanding
**hoard** *v.* to collect, store, or hide a large amount of something (often secretly)
**germ** *n.* a tiny living thing that can cause illness
**phobia** *n.* an irrational fear of something

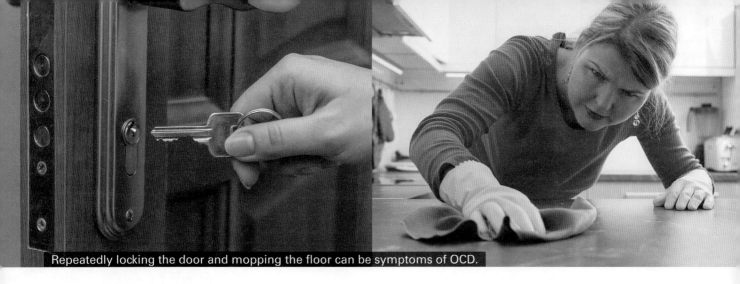
Repeatedly locking the door and mopping the floor can be symptoms of OCD.

are a kind of anxiety disorder. This family of mental disorders also includes social anxiety disorder, panic disorder, and post-traumatic stress disorder (PTSD). While the majority of anxiety disorders relate to fears about present or future events, the last condition is triggered by a traumatic event in the past. Triggers might include extreme situations such as war, accidents, and child abuse. As with other anxiety disorders, there are a variety of treatments available for PTSD, including psychotherapy and sustained support from family and friends.

Phobias and OCD are similar in terms of the way irrational fear impacts behavior. Both conditions involve obsessions, and phobias also sometimes involve a degree of compulsion. Imagine, for example, you are terrified of cockroaches. You see one scuttling across the bedroom floor and, after that, you cannot get the image of the disgusting creature out of your mind. You're becoming obsessed. Soon, you're looking under the bed, turning over your pillows and shaking the sheets out to ensure there are no unwelcome surprises when it's time for bed. Now you're getting compulsive.

So, why is this not a prime example of OCD? The key difference is that a person suffering from OCD will be racked by strong feelings that something dreadful will happen if they don't act to prevent it. For example—as bizarre as it seems—they may be convinced that the cockroach will cause serious harm to them or their family. In addition, an OCD sufferer's compulsive behavior will usually take the form of a ritual. This means the pillow turning and sheet shaking will almost always proceed in exactly the same order and in exactly the same fashion. OCD fears might make a person continually lock and unlock doors and windows to check they are secure. Terrified that his or her family could be exposed to burglars or other dangers, the OCD sufferer feels compelled to repeat the routine. While some

## Notes

**psychotherapy**  *n.*  the treatment of mental disorder through discussion rather than the use of medicine
**cockroach**  *n.*  a large dark-colored insect often found where food is stored or prepared
**scuttle**  *v.*  to run rapidly with short steps (often used by small creatures)
**bizarre**  *adj.*  extremely odd or strange

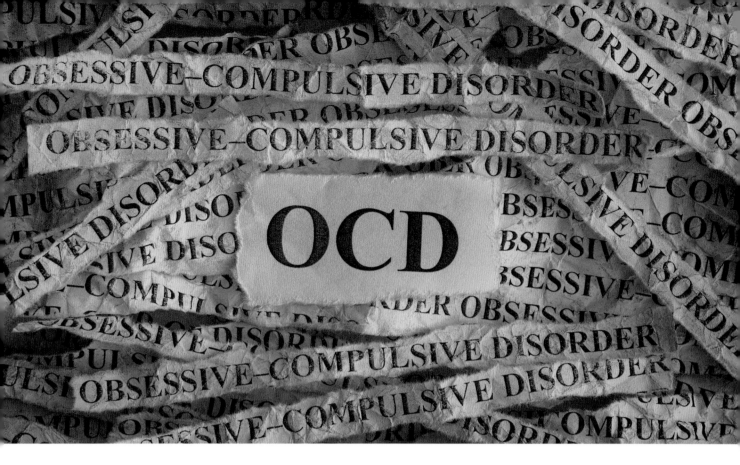

OCD types might have no limit to the repetitions, others may have a certain number they need to achieve before they feel comfortable. Perhaps the worst type of OCD is the fear that you yourself might harm friends or family. This can make the sufferer's life unbearable and lead to severe depression and suicidal thoughts.

All of this brings us back to that other set of letters we saw in the first paragraph of this article, for these provide a solution to OCD. One of the biggest problems for OCD sufferers is a lack of understanding regarding their condition. Normal psychotherapy rarely works for OCD. Talking about the anxiety does not help as these are not rational fears. In fact, evidence suggests discussion and attempts to reassure sufferers can actually make things worse. The most effective way to combat OCD is to tackle it head-on through a method known as "exposure and response prevention." This strategy is necessarily cruel. A person obsessed with germs, for instance, may be forced to touch the toilet seat. In extreme cases, people may be asked to fully submerge their hands in the water of the toilet bowl. After that, they will be told not to wash their hands.

As mean as this process sounds, OCD sufferers swear by it. Many people who have had their lives almost ruined by OCD believe that ERP is the only way to truly overcome the condition. This makes sense. After all, it is only by confronting these irrational fears that one can conquer them.

## Reading Comprehension

**Multiple Choice:** Based on the reading, choose the best answer to each question.

**FIGURATIVE LANGUAGE**

1. In Line 9, the expression "way off the mark" is closest in meaning to _____.
   a. absolutely correct
   b. extremely stupid
   c. totally confusing
   d. completely mistaken

**DETAIL**

2. What is true about OCD sufferers?
   a. They rarely act out their obsessions.
   b. They are always both obsessive and compulsive.
   c. They don't always engage in compulsive behavior.
   d. They sometimes lack obsessive thoughts.

**DETAIL**

3. What does the author say about the frequency with which OCD sufferers might wash their hands?
   a. There might be a short gap between each time they do it.
   b. There might be a course of days between each time they do it.
   c. There might be a long gap between each time they think about it.
   d. There might be an interval between the time they think about it and the time they do it.

**DETAIL**

4. What is NOT mentioned as a difference between phobias and OCD?
   a. OCD involves doing things in the same order.
   b. OCD involves a fear that something bad will happen.
   c. OCD involves bugs and other creatures.
   d. OCD involves doing things a certain number of times.

**DETAIL**

5. Why is psychotherapy NOT an effective way to treat OCD?
   a. Because OCD sufferers cannot explain why they have their negative ideas
   b. Because OCD sufferers are afraid of talking about their fears
   c. Because OCD sufferers do not like psychotherapy
   d. Because OCD sufferers need to be reassured

**PHRASE**

6. In Line 69, what does the author mean by saying "OCD sufferers swear by it"?
   a. They think ERP is too extreme.
   b. They are confident that ERP is useful.
   c. They strongly resist using ERP.
   d. They believe psychotherapy is better than ERP.

**Think More**

1. What do you think of the ERP method? Is it the only way to help people overcome their fears?

2. Why do you think some people act out their obsessions while others don't?

## Reading Skill | Scanning for Abbreviations

Abbreviations can include acronyms and initialisms. The former are words that are formed from the first letters in a phrase or a word. Sometimes these acronyms become so well known that many people do not even know what the original words are. One example is the word *laser*, which stands for "light amplification by stimulated emission of radiation." Like acronyms, initialisms are groups of letters that stand for individual words. However, they are not usually pronounced as words. The initials *USB*, standing for "universal serial bus," would be an example. When you see an unfamiliar abbreviation, try to scan the text around it to see if there are any further explanations that may help you to understand it.

**Task 1:** Read the following short passage. Circle the abbreviations and underline their full versions in the text.

In today's news, the National Aeronautics and Space Administration has announced that one of its astronauts reported seeing an unidentified flying object in outer space last Friday. NASA has not yet made any further comments regarding this claim. However, other interested groups and organizations are looking forward to receiving more news about this UFO.

**Task 2:** Scan Reading and answer the following questions.

1. What does ERP stand for? _____

2. What does PTSD stand for? _____

## Vocabulary Builder | The Root Word *sure*

A root word is the form of a word after all prefixes or suffixes are removed. It holds the most basic meaning of the word. For example, in Reading, we saw the verbs *ensure* and *reassure*. The root word of these words is *sure*. They have a similar basic meaning (i.e. to make an outcome certain or sure); however, they also have distinct meanings of their own.

**Task 1:** Match the following words to the most appropriate definitions.

1. insure      •
2. ensure      •
3. assure      •
4. reassure    •

• to calm someone or make them less worried
• to tell someone that something is definitely true
• to arrange for a payment in case of damage or injury
• to make certain something will happen

**Task 2:** Choose a verb from Task 1 to complete the following sentences. Change the word form if necessary.

1. No matter what happens, I can _____ you that I will always love you.

2. My cousin is very nervous about going traveling alone, but I have done my best to _____ her.

3. Can you _____ that the goods will arrive on time? We can't afford any delays.

4. When Leyla injured herself and had to spend a month in hospital, she was glad she had _____ herself.

# OBSESSIVE-COMPULSIVE DISORDER

## Let's Think About It!

With a partner, find out what the following phobias are and what characteristics or symptoms a person may have if he or she has them. Then, work with your partner to come up with some possible suggestions about how to handle these phobias. Of course, a phobia is irrational and difficult to deal with, but you can do your best to provide some suggestions that might be helpful. Finally, discuss with your partner if you or he/she suffers from any type of phobia and write down the key points in the final boxes below.

| Phobia | Characteristics/Symptoms | Suggestions |
|---|---|---|
| Aerophobia | • Fear of being on an airplane <br> • Trying to avoid travel by plane as much as possible <br> • Feeling uncomfortable when sitting in a plane or even when thinking about flying | • Take deep breaths to relax <br> • Use virtual reality equipment to expose the person with aerophobia to a safe flying environment and let him/her get used to it |
| Bacteriophobia | | |
| Acrophobia | | |
| Claustrophobia | | |
| | | |

# Review 2 (Units 7–12)

## I. Definition Matching

*Match the words to the correct definitions.*

1. insecure •          • to begin suddenly or break out

2. erupt •          • a shortened version of a word or phrase

3. linger •          • to stay somewhere too long

4. sensitivity •          • not feeling confident about oneself

5. abbreviation •          • showing an understanding and awareness of other people's thoughts or feelings

## II. Sentence Completion

*Choose the correct words to complete the sentences.*

1. The comedian was known for being able to _____ many famous celebrities.
   a. mimic          b. anticipate          c. confuse          d. identify

2. A rise in extreme weather in the future, such as droughts and floods, could lead to increased instances of _____ on a global scale.
   a. famine          b. livestock          c. wildlife          d. produce

3. The overuse of plastic bags will _____ lead to environmental pollution.
   a. in all          b. in turn          c. in case          d. in advance

4. It's not a good idea to walk _____ on the street; there could be bits of broken glass.
   a. casually          b. underfoot          c. barefoot          d. virtually

5. Yesterday I bought a big _____ for all my clothes.
   a. wardrobe          b. turnover          c. pact          d. trait

6. In tropical countries, farmers often have to use a high level of _____ to kill harmful insects.
   a. pesticides          b. garments          c. turnovers          d. catwalks

7. The brand's logo is very _____ and easy to recognize.
   a. distinctive          b. imminent          c. optimistic          d. industrial

8. The broken bone was easy to _____ as it showed up clearly on the X-ray.
   a. unfold          b. diagnose          c. render          d. decide

9. I found the loud music _____, so I told my neighbor to turn it down.
   a. unbearable          b. external          c. passing          d. irrational

10. Jerry had a car accident last December. Luckily, he _____ himself, so he didn't have to spend his own money fixing his car.
    a. ensured          b. insured          c. assured          d. reassured

## III. Cloze Test

*Choose the correct words to complete the passages.*

**A**  2-49

A lack of clean, drinkable water has been pegged as the world's next big crisis. But for many people, the lack of this basic ___1___ for life isn't some far-off catastrophe. From their ___2___, it's already here. For example, in Nigeria, the supply of clean water has long been ___3___. In a population of 192 million, around 60 million Nigerians live without access to safe drinking water. Even water-rich nations are not immune. Brazil, for example, has 12 percent of the world's fresh water. And yet, the vital resource has been managed so poorly that the government has had to ___4___ people to ration water in their homes. If nations where water is plentiful already have to limit their ___5___, it serves as a stern warning that we must take this problem more seriously, and the sooner the better.

1. a. paradox     b. habitat     c. necessity     d. famine
2. a. plea     b. terrorism     c. perspective     d. livestock
3. a. imminent     b. insufficient     c. equivalent     d. inefficient
4. a. call upon     b. call down     c. call in     d. call up
5. a. distraction     b. invention     c. consumption     d. inspection

**B**  2-50

These days, many clothing brands use words like "sustainable" or "organic" to describe their products. Their aim is to create the image of a(n) ___1___ brand that does not harm the environment. However, in many cases, there is really no ___2___ difference between these brands and other clothing companies. So, how can we know for sure which brands are really trustworthy when it comes to doing the right thing? Well, the short answer is that we can't always be sure. We can still be ___3___, though. Some companies are really making ___4___ progress in providing clothing that doesn't have a negative impact. One such brand is Krochet Kids. This non-profit company employs workers in Uganda and Peru who are trained for three years and guaranteed a fair wage. Each handmade ___5___ is signed, indicating who made it.

1. a. reluctant     b. resistant     c. hazardous     d. ethical
2. a. noticeable     b. soothing     c. responsible     d. ideal
3. a. psychiatric     b. invasive     c. optimistic     d. dreadful
4. a. vulnerable     b. remarkable     c. acceptable     d. stoppable
5. a. trait     b. garment     c. pact     d. notion

## IV. Reading Comprehension

*Read the articles and choose the correct answers.*

 **A**  2-51

In recent years, climate change has become such a serious problem that many people think the environment is already beyond saving. However, there are still ways to save the natural world. One of the most feasible ways is to cut down on how much meat you eat, or even go vegetarian or vegan.

The largest study of the global meat industry to date has revealed a few startling facts. Published in the journal *Science*, the study found that although livestock provides the world population with just 18 percent of its calories, it takes up 83 percent of the world's farmland. Furthermore, the meat and dairy industry produces 60 percent of agriculture's greenhouse gases, which contribute to global climate change.

If the world were to do away with meat and dairy farms altogether, the study also claims, global farmland could be cut down by three-quarters. To put that in perspective, that would be an area equivalent to the combined size of the US, China, the European Union and Australia. This land could be converted back to nature and provide a safe haven for endangered species. Not to mention that the land could also have trees and other vegetation planted on it again, and those plants would in turn recycle the vast amounts of carbon dioxide that have caused the global temperature to rise.

So, if you're looking to make a change to help the environment, don't forget that your diet plays an important role not only in your health, but in the health of the planet as well.

1. What is the main point of this article?
   a. A change in your diet can have a major impact.
   b. Cutting down on carbon dioxide is the most important thing.
   c. The environment is hard to save.
   d. Eating more meat is beneficial for us all.

2. What is true about livestock, according to the article?
   a. It increases world population by 18 percent.
   b. It helps lower the global temperature.
   c. It provides few calories to the world, but takes up much of the farmland.
   d. Fewer livestock can save endangered animals.

3. According to the passage, what would be the cause of global farmland being cut by 75 percent?
   a. A global shift to an all-meat diet
   b. An increase in the amount of greenhouse gases
   c. A rise in the global temperature
   d. The elimination of meat and dairy farms

4. What can we infer about the amount of land taken up by meat and dairy farming globally?
   a. It could just barely cover the United States.
   b. It is enough to cover more than one continent.
   c. It is the size of a small nation.
   d. It is the size of a few major cities.

5. What percentage of greenhouse gases does the meat and dairy industry produce?
   a. 18 percent       b. 60 percent
   c. 75 percent       d. 83 percent

**B**

Postnatal depression (PND) is a well documented condition in women. As early as 700 B.C., the Greek physician Hippocrates discussed the issue of women experiencing emotional difficulties after childbirth. The "father of medicine," as he is sometimes known, recognized that certain women had problems after childbirth.

However, it wasn't until 2,500 years later that modern doctors finally began to take these issues seriously. Even then, most doctors did not believe that their patients were genuinely depressed. Instead, they thought these women were exaggerating their feelings and being **neurotic**. Some professionals even believed PND sufferers were insane.

The view that some new mothers were simply emotionally unstable continued for much of the 20th century. Up until the 1950s, treatments like electroshock therapy were prescribed to "cure" overly emotional women. Most women were too scared or embarrassed to talk about their experiences because of the social stigma attached. After all, what kind of woman could be unhappy about having a child? Finally, by the 1980s, this PND was recognized and diagnosed as a real form of depression. At last, women began to receive the treatment they needed.

Symptoms of PND include anxiety, a severe lack of energy, major mood swings, tears for no particular reason, and changes to sleeping and eating patterns. At its worst, PND could lead to thoughts of harming oneself or the newborn child. Psychotherapy or counseling is recommended as the best form of help, though antidepressant medication is sometimes prescribed. Whatever happens, women suffering from PND should know that help is at hand. The bad old days of treating PND as an emotional overreaction are firmly behind us.

1. What is true about Hippocrates?
   a. He was a famous Greek doctor.
   b. His wife suffered from PND.
   c. He did not believe PND was real.
   d. He created a famous brand of medicine.

2. In the second paragraph, the word "neurotic" is closest in meaning to _____.
   a. completely insane
   b. really depressed
   c. emotionally unstable
   d. absolutely genuine

3. In the third paragraph, why does the author ask the question "what kind of woman could be unhappy about having a child?"
   a. To show his or her own surprise at such behavior
   b. To emphasize that such behavior is not considered normal by society
   c. To tell the reader that this kind of behavior is unacceptable
   d. To show sympathy toward women who suffer from PND

4. What is NOT mentioned as a symptom of PND?
   a. Having trouble eating and sleeping
   b. Crying without a clear cause
   c. Thoughts of violence
   d. Fear of certain types of medicine

5. What is the main idea of the article?
   a. PND is a serious issue that should not be taken lightly.
   b. Doctors have yet to realize the seriousness of PND.
   c. Patients are still scared to admit that they suffer from PND.
   d. Attitudes toward PND are a lot different now than in the past.

## TEXT PRODUCTION STAFF

edited by 編集
Takashi Kudo 工藤 隆志

cover design by 表紙デザイン
Nobuyoshi Fujino 藤野 伸芳

DTP by DTP
ALIUS (Hiroyuki Kinouchi) アリウス (木野内 宏行)

## CD PRODUCTION STAFF

recorded by 吹き込み者
Rachel Walzer (AmE) レイチェル・ワルザー (アメリカ英語)
Bill Sullivan (AmE) ビル・サリバン (アメリカ英語)

## Flow: Reading Without Borders
### 読解力強化のためのスタイル別リーディング演習

2023年1月20日　初版発行
2023年2月15日　第2刷発行

著　　者　　James Baron
　　　　　　Joe Henley

発 行 者　　佐野 英一郎

発 行 所　　株式会社 成 美 堂
　　　　　　〒101-0052　東京都千代田区神田小川町3-22
　　　　　　TEL 03-3291-2261　FAX 03-3293-5490
　　　　　　https://www.seibido.co.jp

印 刷・製 本　　三美印刷株式会社

ISBN 978-4-7919-7273-9　　　　　　　　　　　　　　Printed in Japan